TOTEM
POLES

TOTEM POLES

WRITTEN & ILLUSTRATED BY
HILARY STEWART

University of Washington Press
Seattle

University of Washington Press
P.O. Box 50096
Seattle, WA 98145-5096

Published simultaneously in Canada by
Douglas & McIntyre Ltd.
1615 Venables Street
Vancouver, British Columbia V5L 2H1

Library of Congress Cataloging-in-Publication Data
Stewart, Hilary
    Totem poles / written and illustrated by Hilary Stewart.
        p.   cm.
    Includes bibliographical references and index.
    ISBN 0-295-97052-9
    1. Totem poles—Northwest Coast of North America.
2. Indians of North America—Northwest Coast of North
America—Sculpture.
I. Title
E98.T6574   1990   90-12614
730′.89′970711--dc20

Editing by Saeko Usukawa
Design by Barbara Hodgson
Front jacket photograph by Rick Marotz/Image Finders. Detail of a
    totem pole by Bill Reid, Museum of Anthropology, University of
    British Columbia, Vancouver, B.C.

Typeset by The Typeworks
Printed and bound in Canada by D. W. Friesen & Sons Ltd.
Printed on acid-free paper ∞

Financially assisted by the Ministry of Municipal Affairs, Recreation
and Culture through the British Columbia Heritage Trust and
British Columbia Lotteries.

CONTENTS

LIST OF MAPS

PREFACE

Standing on the beach under a grey sky, I watched with apprehension as dozens of strong arms heaved on two ropes to raise the tall totem pole, little by little, to a vertical position in front of the plank house. To prevent the sideways sway of the pole on its upward journey, two teams of people held two other ropes taut.

The crowd stood in anxious silence, watching—the hush a contrast to the drumming and speech making that had preceded the pole raising. As I moved up from the beach, closer to the plank house, one of the hauling ropes bit into the cedar shakes at the roof edge and jammed. Two men on the roof ripped away the offending shakes and freed the rope. I heard it creaking from the strain of pulling up the massive log until a final heave brought the pole upright against the house front. A sudden burst of cheering and furious drumming shattered the silent tension, expressing the jubilation of about a thousand residents and offshore visitors.

The two-day celebration that followed featured a lavish potlatch—with dancing, singing, drumming, speeches, feasting and gift giving—for all who had witnessed this very special event. I felt privileged to have been invited.

The year was 1978, the place was Skidegate on the Queen Charlotte Islands, and the carver of the pole was Bill Reid. It was the first pole to be raised in the village in more than a hundred years, and only the second on the islands in the last decade.

With the regeneration of native art and tradition spreading throughout the Northwest Coast since the late 1960s, the proliferation of new totem poles has been remarkable.

Perhaps no other product of Northwest Coast creativity is as well known as the totem pole; it has become the very symbol of Northwest Coast Indian people and their art, provincially, nationally and around the world. Although the name "totem" for these carved monuments of cedar is actually a misnomer—a totem is a creature or object that a person holds in great respect and religious awe—many years of common usage and the want of a better word have made it acceptable. Similarly, the word "chief," although an inexact translation, has been given validity through common usage, particularly by native people themselves.

The majority of totem poles on view today are not in context. Many have been placed along highways; at ferry terminals; in parks, gardens and shopping plazas; outside hotels, public buildings, tourist bureaus, schools and, of course, in museums. Visitors to the Northwest Coast from all parts of the world often stand in wonder before some of the largest wooden sculptures ever created, astounded by their height and girth. They are perplexed and intrigued by the bold, complex designs and the extraordinary creatures of strange proportions that emerge from the logs with such vitality; and they ask, "What are they and what do they mean?" Most poles are accompanied by the barest information or none at all. Questions about what kind of wood, who the carver was, how long it took to carve, how old it is, how it was raised and what the figures represent are mainly left unanswered.

This book attempts to satisfy that curiosity while adding cultural and historic background as well as human interest. In addition to explaining the different types of poles, their function and symbolism, this book relates legends associated with many of the carved figures. The totem poles illustrated are all outdoors, are readily accessible (with one exception), and for the most part are in places frequented by visitors.

Three years of travel and research have revealed an unexpectedly large number of poles—far too many to include all of them in this book. In some areas with a major group of poles, I have chosen to illustrate only a few. Due to space limitations, several good poles that I would have liked to include have been left out; some poles of lesser quality have been included for special reasons. Poles whose paint is weathered away are illustrated as though newly painted.

Two villages in northern British Columbia, Kitwanga and Kitwancool, both off the beaten track, with fine stands of old and replaced poles well worth visiting, did not wish to be included in the book, and I have respected that.

Rather than grouping together poles from the same cultural area, I have presented them by location in a geographic sequence that will be useful to the traveller. Starting at the southern border of British Columbia, the route covers the Vancouver area, Sechelt and Vancouver Island, with side trips to Quadra Island and Alert Bay. The route then continues north to Port Hardy and the Queen Charlotte Islands, back to the mainland and Prince Rupert, inland along the Skeena River valley, then west into Alaska to Ketchikan, and north to Juneau and Wrangell.

Instead of giving measurements for the heights of poles, I have included scales or diagrammatic figures (which represent 1.8 m or 6 feet) to give a better idea of the proportion; this does not include the base on which the pole stands, if there is one, unless it is shown in the illustration.

Etiquette requires that no one should lean against, sit on or climb totem poles—much less carve initials, pry off a souvenir, or in any way deface a pole or its setting. While Indian villages are in fact private property, generally the residents do not mind visitors who are respectful and considerate of their surroundings. Photographing the totem poles is permitted, but some villages have restrictions on the commercial use of the photos. Check with the band office if the photos are not for personal use.

Totem poles, whether old or new, in their original setting or not, are unique to the Pacific Northwest Coast of North America. The statement they make goes beyond the carver's art and the history they embody. The message is timeless, for such is the commitment to continuing growth and strength by the first people of this land—the people of the poles.

As always with my books, research is a lengthy and time-consuming process that relies, in large measure, on the kindness and generosity of a broad spectrum of people.

I am most appreciative of all those who have given of their knowledge and expertise to assist me with historical and local information, and with ethnographical, anthropological and linguistic data.

My warmest thanks go to those who provided or assisted with photographic material; who searched library shelves and archives; who loaned me books, articles and papers, and who phoned, wrote or met with me to answer my questions.

My sincere thanks to those who accompanied me on distant travels or gave me shelter, sustenance and encouragement on my research journeys.

To the individuals, elders, chiefs, band managers, museum directors and officials of various institutions, companies and municipalities who gave me permission to include their totem poles in this book—my thanks.

I am particularly indebted to the many carvers who discussed their work with me, and to those who provided not only information on the crests and stories behind the sculptured figures but also contributed personal anecdotes pertaining to the cedar monuments they carved.

To the many people—whether listed or not—who made three years of research, writing and illustrating a worthwhile and gratifying time, I would like to offer my sincere appreciation and thanks:

Roxana Adams, Director, Totem Heritage Park, Ketchikan; Dempsey Bob, Tsimshian carver; Cliff Bolton, Band Manager, Kitsumkalum; Lee Boyko, Assistant Director, Museum of Northern British Columbia, Prince Rupert; Steve Brown, carver, Seattle; Simon Charlie, Coast Salish carver, Duncan; Terri Clark, Public Relations, Vancouver Parks Board; Mary Clifton, elder, Comox Band; Dora Sewid Cook, Cape Mudge Band, Quadra Island; Bill Cranmer, Band Manager, Alert Bay; Joe David, Nuu-chah-nulth carver; Claude Davidson, Haida carver; Reg Davidson, Haida carver; Robert Davidson, Haida carver; Sara Davidson, Masset; Freda Diesing, Haida carver; Paul Donville, City Administrator, Duncan; Bill Ellis, Queen Charlotte Islands; Mary Everson, Comox Band; Scott Foster, author, Juneau; Margaret Frank, elder, Comox Band; Deborah Griffiths, Director, Courtenay Museum and Archives; Walter Harris, Gitksan carver; Jim Hart, Haida carver; Bill Henderson, Kwakiutl carver; Dorothy Horner, Gitksan carver; Calvin Hunt, Kwakiutl carver; Richard Hunt, Kwakiutl carver; Tony Hunt, Kwakiutl carver; Joy Inglis, anthropologist, Quadra Island; Richard Inglis, Curator of Ethnology, Royal British Columbia Museum, Victoria; Jamie Jeffries, Coast Salish carver; Doreen Jensen, Gitksan carver; Vickie Jensen, photographer, Vancouver; Norman John, Nuu-chah-nulth carver; Michael Kew, anthropologist, University of British Columbia; Pamela Knapp, Manager, Alaska State Museum, Juneau; Anton Kolstee, Native Student Counsellor, Carson Graham School, North Vancouver; Suellen Liljeblad, Curator, Ketchikan Museum; Jim McDonald, Assistant Curator, Ethnology, Royal Ontario Museum, Toronto; Bud Mintz, Potlatch Arts Ltd., Vancouver; Lyn Miranda, Curator, Vancouver Museum; Earl Muldoe, Gitksan carver; Pete Muldoe, elder, Kispiox; Phil Nuytten, Vancouver; Sandra Parrish, museum technician, Campbell River Museum and Archives; Duane Pasco, carver, Seattle; Thomas Paul, Chief, Sechelt Band; Tim Paul, Nuu-chah-nulth carver; Rose Point, Musqueam Band; Jay Powell, Professor of Linguistics, University of British Columbia; Bill Reid, Haida carver; Chris Robertson, Band Manager, Musqueam; Laura Robertson, Historical Photographs Division, Vancouver Public Library; Marcie Robinson, Vancouver Native Housing; Irene Ross, Archivist-Registrar, Campbell River Museum and Archives; Polly Sargent, Hazelton; Dan Savard, Anthropological Collections, Royal British Columbia Museum, Victoria; Jessica Stephens, Nuu-chah-nulth, teacher, Port Alberni; Jay Stewart, Director, Campbell River Museum and Archives; Peter Stewart, Vernon; Norman Tait, Nishga carver; Art Thompson, Nuu-chah-nulth carver; Margaret Vickers, Band Manager, Kispiox; Rodney Ward, Chairman, Board of Directors, Vancouver Museum; Gloria Webster, Director, U'mista Cultural Centre, Alert Bay; Charlie Wesley, elder, Skidegate; Ellen White, Coast Salish elder, Nanaimo; Alice Wilson, elder, Kispiox; Jane Wilson, Public Relations, Canadian Broadcasting Corporation, Vancouver; Stanley Wilson, elder, Kispiox; Don Yoemans, Haida carver; Joan Zamluk, Campbell River.

PHOTOGRAPH BY HILARY STEWART

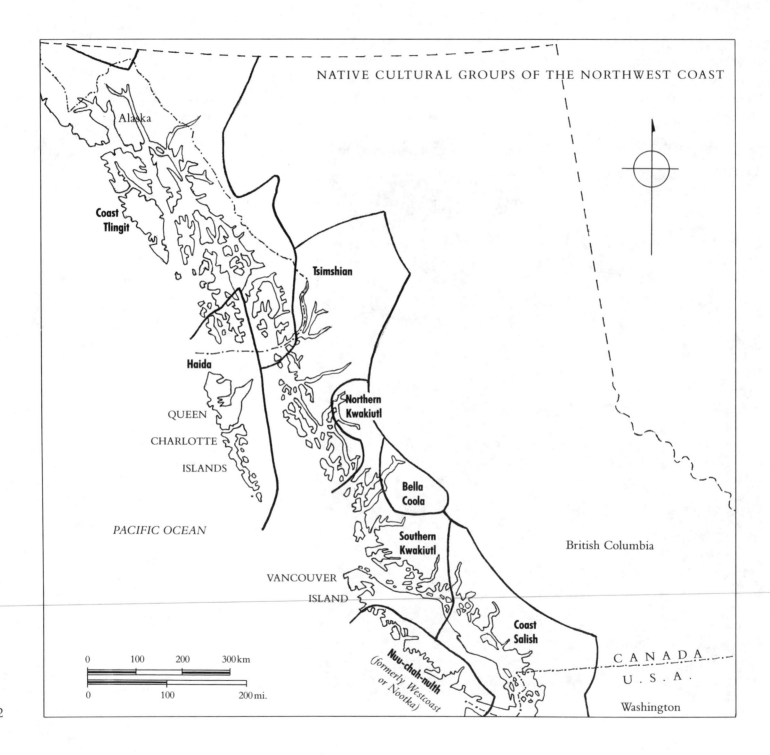

NATIVE CULTURAL GROUPS OF THE NORTHWEST COAST

Alaska

**Coast
Tlingit**

Tsimshian

Haida

QUEEN

CHARLOTTE

ISLANDS

**Northern
Kwakiutl**

**Bella
Coola**

**Southern
Kwakiutl**

PACIFIC OCEAN

British Columbia

VANCOUVER

ISLAND

**Coast
Salish**

0   100   200   300 km

0   100   200 mi.

*Nuu-chah-nulth
(formerly Westcoast
or Nootka)*

C A N A D A

U.S.A.

Washington

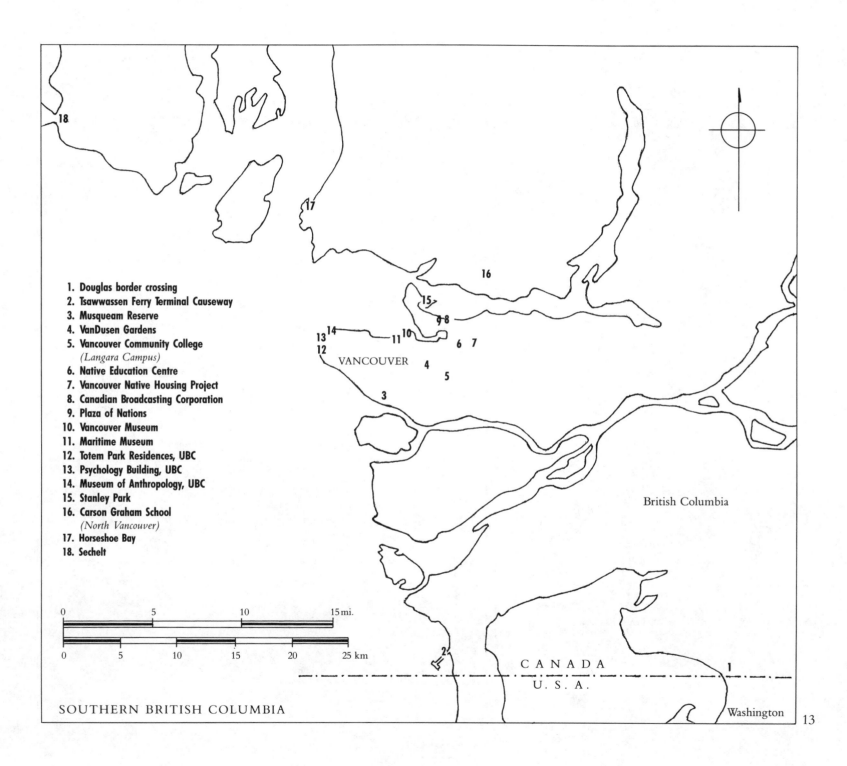

1. Douglas border crossing
2. Tsawwassen Ferry Terminal Causeway
3. Musqueam Reserve
4. VanDusen Gardens
5. Vancouver Community College
   (Langara Campus)
6. Native Education Centre
7. Vancouver Native Housing Project
8. Canadian Broadcasting Corporation
9. Plaza of Nations
10. Vancouver Museum
11. Maritime Museum
12. Totem Park Residences, UBC
13. Psychology Building, UBC
14. Museum of Anthropology, UBC
15. Stanley Park
16. Carson Graham School
    (North Vancouver)
17. Horseshoe Bay
18. Sechelt

VANCOUVER

British Columbia

C A N A D A
U. S. A.

Washington

SOUTHERN BRITISH COLUMBIA

0   5   10   15 mi.

0   5   10   15   20   25 km

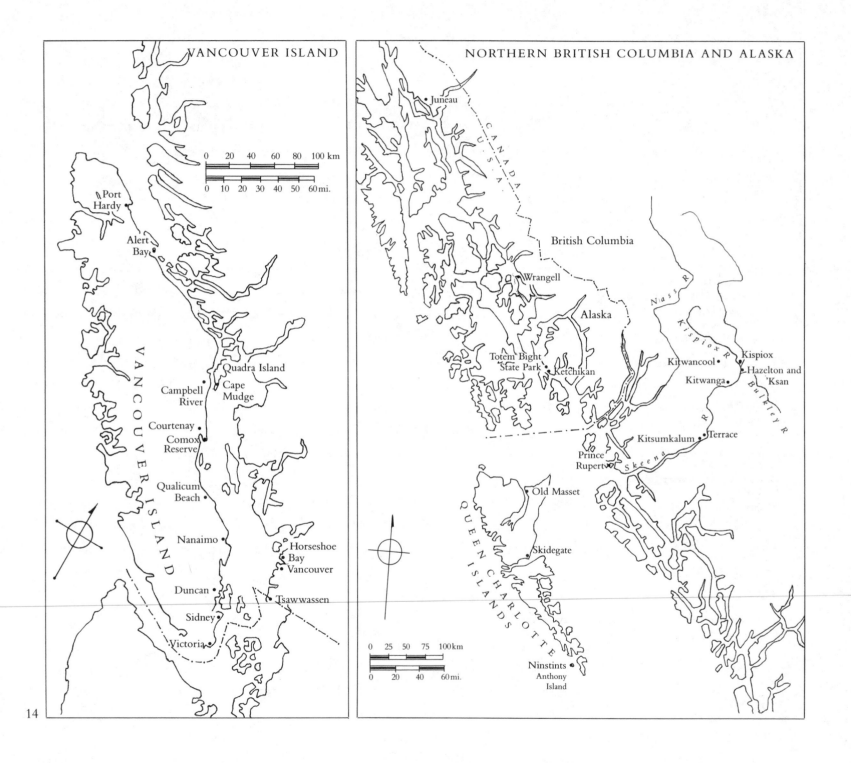

VANCOUVER ISLAND

0 20 40 60 80 100 km

0 10 20 30 40 50 60 mi.

Port Hardy

Alert Bay

Quadra Island

Campbell River

Cape Mudge

Courtenay

Comox Reserve

Qualicum Beach

Nanaimo

Horseshoe Bay

Vancouver

Duncan

Tsawwassen

Sidney

Victoria

V A N C O U V E R   I S L A N D

NORTHERN BRITISH COLUMBIA AND ALASKA

Juneau

British Columbia

Wrangell

Alaska

C A N A D A
U. S. A.

N i a s s   R

Kispiox R

Bulkley R

Totem Bight State Park

Ketchikan

Kitwancool

Kitwanga

Kispiox

Hazelton and 'Ksan

Kitsumkalum

Terrace

Skeena R

Prince Rupert

Old Masset

Q U E E N   C H A R L O T T E   I S L A N D S

Skidegate

Ninstints
Anthony Island

0 25 50 75 100 km

0 20 40 60 mi.

14

PART 1 THE BACKGROUND

THE NORTHWEST COAST: THE LAND AND THE PEOPLE

A vast area of extraordinary beauty, the Pacific Northwest Coast of North America extends some 2000 km (1,300 miles). Its coastline, rugged and spectacular, is deeply indented and broken by countless inlets, channels, bays and rivers, as well as scattered with hundreds of large and small islands. The temperate climate clothes the steep mountains and valley bottoms in a rich profusion of plant life, creating a lush, evergreen rain forest that sweeps to the edge of the sea. Along the foreshore and the banks of the rivers that flow to it, the sea-oriented aboriginal people have made their homes for thousands of years.

Hunters and gatherers, they harvested their food from land, sea and intertidal zone, taking a variety of fish, sea mammals, mollusks, land mammals, wild fowl and vegetation. The wood of conifer and deciduous trees, grasses, rushes, bark and roots, together with animal furs, hides, bones and antlers, as well as shells and stones, provided the raw materials for all their daily and ceremonial needs. Sea-going and river canoes assured access to most of the resources, while a network of trading increased the availability of other foods and materials.

The native people were, in fact, seven distinct nations (loosely termed tribes), speaking different languages and many dialects; their customs, practices and art styles varied from north to south, but they also held much in common. They were a civilization with an elaborate social and ceremonial structure, and with traditions that were said to go back to the beginning of time. They sited their villages in sheltered bays and inlets, and lived in large, sturdy post and beam houses that provided warmth and comfort. Each household consisted of several families, all related, and each family had an assigned place in the house. Boxes of stored foods, wealth goods and ceremonial regalia, as well as tools and implements, were stacked against the walls.

Wealth and prestige, achievement and high rank, were linked to family lineage, history and possession of rights. Marriage between various groups strengthened the bonds of alliance, adding security from the threat of belligerence. The head of a household was a chief, and his close relatives were the nobles. More distant relatives and any others in the tribe were the commoners, with slaves and their

Dancers in button blankets play an important role in the potlatch, as do drumming and singing. PHOTOGRAPH BY HILARY STEWART

offspring ranking last. The most powerful, highest-ranking chief of all the households was chief of the village.

The people's understanding of the interconnectedness of all living things and their dependence on certain animal and plant species fostered belief in the supernatural and spirit world. Life forms, especially those taken for food and other uses, each had their own spirit. To show these spirits respect ensured their continued return or regrowth in the years ahead.

Certain birds and animals were associated with particular behaviours, powers or skills, and people sought their help to achieve success in endeavours such as fishing, whaling or hunting. But evil spirits and mythic creatures with powers to harm and bring death also roamed abroad, threatening the vulnerable. Spirit experiences and encounters held great significance, and tales of these were recalled and passed on to each generation.

In the dark of long winter nights, when fires burned in the centres of the big plank houses and smoke rose up through openings in the roofs, then the spirits drew close to the village. It was a time of special ceremonies, speeches, singing, dancing and feasting; of reaffirming family identities, rights and properties. The people's spirituality ran deep and their sense of identity was strong. Through costumed spiritual transformations and re-enactments, they brought past histories and adventures into the present. Thus, the carved beings of crest and legend portrayed on the totem poles, often recreated in masks worn by dancers, sprang to life.

When the winter dances and ceremonies ended, the sculptured poles in front of the houses continued to confirm who dwelt there and how they ranked in society.

The raising of a totem pole—and other important events such as birth, marriage, death, the completion of a new house, the acquisition of a new crest, the transfer of property, or the succession of a new chief—were marked by the giving of a ceremony called a potlatch. The word "potlatch," now used by all the native groups along the entire Northwest Coast, originated with the Nuu-chah-nulth word *pa-chitle*, meaning "to give." But giving was only one aspect of this most important and complex social occasion around which the culture revolved.

While the potlatch commemorated an event, it was also a time to mourn deaths since the previous potlatch, initiate novices into "secret societies", repay outstanding debts, and bestow hereditary names on young people. For a people who had no written documentation, the potlatch was a way of publicly acknowledging and validating events before witnesses. Invited well ahead of time, people came from many villages, often travelling long distances by canoe.

A potlatch was expensive in terms of labour, foodstuffs and material goods given out, and it often took years of preparation by the host family, with support from relatives, to accumulate the necessary supplies. Thus only a wealthy family could give a potlatch.

A high-ranking person could maintain or increase his power and status through the extravagance of his potlatch, especially if it surpassed that of a rival chief. He displayed his wealth, which took the form of crests, names, stories, songs, dances, masks, heirlooms and other properties, as well as certain rights and privileges. The ownership of natural resources also indicated wealth: salmon streams, hunting lands, berry-gathering places, stands of cedar, clam-digging beaches and so on, and ownership of these would be confirmed in boastful speeches.

Feasting on a grand scale formed an important part of the potlatch, with hundreds of guests being fed and housed for days, often weeks. The giving of gifts to all those present not only represented payment for witnessing but also served to reaffirm each guest's rank and status, since the value of a gift had to be in proportion to the recipient's social standing. At the conclusion of the potlatch, the obligatory food surplus was distributed to guests to take home. Some of it provided sustenance on the journey home, and the rest was shared with others of the village.

A lavish potlatch would be talked about for a long time, enhancing the status of the host and his family—and it is much the same today.

Some family poles raised long ago are still in place today. Others, more recently raised, stand in a drastically changed world. But all of them proudly and publicly proclaim family lineage, achievements and rights.

Inside a traditional dance house during a potlatch. A painted screen is stretched between elaborately carved and painted house posts that support a crossbeam. Dancers in crested button blankets circle the floor, to the accompaniment of drumming and singing, Alert Bay, 1981.
PHOTOGRAPH BY HILARY STEWART

TOTEM POLES: A HISTORICAL OVERVIEW

The first white men to set foot on the shores of the Pacific Northwest Coast, in what is now called British Columbia, were invited into the large plank house of a high-ranking chief. The year was 1778, and explorer Capt. James Cook went ashore with his ship's officers and the expedition's official artist, John Webber. Webber, intrigued by the extraordinary carved wood columns that supported the massive roof beams inside the house, set to work drawing them. His illustration, published as an engraving in Cook's three-volume *A Voyage to the Pacific Ocean*, was the first glimpse the people of Europe had of the carved wood columns of the Pacific Northwest Coast Indian peoples.

Describing these huge house posts, Cook wrote in his journal that "many of them are decorated with images. These are nothing more than trunks of very large trees . . . set up singly, or by pairs, at the upper end of the appartment, with the front carved into a human face; the arms and hands cut out upon the sides, and variously painted; so that the whole was a truly monstrous figure."

Another sighting appears in the journal of Capt. George Dixon's explorations of the Queen Charlotte Islands in the early 1790s. He described native art as "figures which might be taken for a species of hieroglyphics: fishes and other animals, heads of men and various whimsical designs, are mingled and confounded in order to compose a subject . . . yet they are not deficient in a sort of elegance and perfection."

Around that time, in 1792, seaman John Bartlett, on board the sailing ship *Gustavus* trading in the Queen Charlotte Islands, wrote in his journal: "We went ashore where one of their winter houses stood. The entrance was cut out of a large tree and carved all the way up and down. The door was made like a man's head and the passage into the house was between his teeth." So impressed was he by the carved tree in the Langara Island village that he later attempted a sketch of it—no doubt from memory—to support his description. Although crudely done, it is the first known drawing of a totem pole standing outdoors.

Although explorers and early traders kept journals, often with detailed descriptions of their observations of the land and the native people, few mentioned carved monuments of wood in the villages, which suggests that such art works were not abundant at the time. Nor has the antiquity for carved poles, either inside or outside the house, been established; but certainly they held significance for the house and its occupants.

These carved monuments were the prerogative of distinguished nobility. The expansion of the fur trade along the northern coast, mainly in sea otter furs, brought increasing wealth to the villages; and with that wealth came the means and the opportunity for nobles to achieve greater status. The noble class acquired more rights and privileges, which meant more and bigger potlatches and elaborate ceremonies to publicly validate these, and the building of larger houses for the ceremonies. As newly rich chiefs competed with one another for prestige and status, skilled carvers were in demand to create taller and more complex poles. Totem poles and the concept of this type of wealth display spread inland up the Skeena River for 240 km (150 miles) and south down the coast to the Kwakiutl and the Nuu-chah-nulth. Northern villages, more than anywhere else, bristled with an astounding array of these monumental art works of high quality and craftsmanship. Many houses had several poles, while some major villages boasted over seventy.

This surge of wealth and its accompanying burst of creativity peaked in the mid-1860s. Then the decline set in. Diminishing numbers of sea otter furs reduced wealth; at the same time, intertribal wars fought with the new deadly European firearms, and new devastating European diseases (particularly smallpox), drastically reduced the native population along the entire coast and inland areas. Many villages, their populations decimated, were abandoned. Missionaries moved in and their Christian indoctrinations increasingly persuaded the people to relinquish their old beliefs and traditions. As a result, totem poles were felled, sold, or even cut up for firewood. Children, wrenched from their families, were sent off to boarding schools and forbidden to speak their own language.

In 1884 the Canadian government outlawed the potlatch, and with it went the very heart of the culture and the need for feast bowls and ladles, masks, headdresses, and all manner of dance and ceremonial regalia and props, and the display of wealth goods. Carvers died without passing on their knowledge to the next generation, and the art reached a low ebb. A few people made miniature totem poles to sell to visitors or to stores. Some of the early pieces were of high quality, but later carvings lacked the dynamic principles of the traditional art style. There were some exceptions. Because potlatching had gone "underground" in many Southern Kwakiutl villages, the arts and traditions there fared better than elsewhere—a circumstance that became of vital importance in later years.

The first known illustration of an exterior totem pole, drawn by John Bartlett, who was trading in the Queen Charlotte Islands in 1792. AUTHOR'S COLLECTION

The great museums of Europe and America sent collectors to the Northwest Coast to reap all the ethnographic artifacts they could persuade the native people to part with, and dealers competed with each other in the scramble to acquire the best pieces at the cheapest prices. Between the 1870s and the 1920s, hundreds of poles were purchased or simply removed from seasonally vacant or abandoned villages without permission or payment. Totem poles were shipped to Washington D.C., Chicago, New York, London, Berlin, Paris and even to New Zealand. Museums in eastern Canada, in Ottawa, Montreal and Toronto, also acquired a share of the treasure; western Canada was as yet too young to have a museum capable of displaying totem poles.

In 1925 the Canadian government and the Canadian National Railway began a restoration project for totem poles still remaining in several Upper Skeena River villages; leaning and fallen poles were set up straight, some facing the highway instead of the river, and painted in bright colours. A United States government project in Alaska from 1938 to 1940 moved many poles from the old abandoned villages; repaired and repainted, the poles were clustered in groups for tourists to view and photograph.

By the late 1920s, anthropologist Marius Barbeau wrote of the poles he had been documenting in the Upper Skeena River: "This art now belongs to the past . . . totem poles are no longer being made."

In British Columbia, the final harvest of standing—and fallen—poles took place in 1957, when several fine poles were collected from Ninstints, a long abandoned village on a remote island off the west coast of the Queen Charlotte Islands. Although these went to museums in Vancouver and Victoria, they at least remained on the Northwest Coast. In the United States, a good number of old poles from the abandoned village sites of Tongass, Village Island (Cat Island) and Old Kasaan were collected in 1970 and are now in Ketchikan's Totem Heritage Center.

Defying an unjust law, some Southern Kwakiutl people continued to potlatch in secret, in remote villages away from government authorities. A few carvers continued to create masks, feast dishes and other items required for potlatches. The best-known carver was Charlie James, born in 1867, who taught his skills to his stepson, Mungo Martin. He also taught his young granddaughter, Ellen, how to carve in cedar, and by age twelve she was making little totem poles to sell to tourists. Married and living in Vancouver in the late 1940s, Ellen Neel developed a thriving business carving miniature totem poles for the tourist trade. When she and her family carved several full-size poles on commission, they made newspaper headlines. But in general, the arts and skills of Northwest Coast people had reached a low point, and the future of their culture was in jeopardy.

In 1950, a major and far-reaching renewal of the art began with a totem pole restoration project at the University of British Columbia's Museum of Anthropology. It employed Mungo Martin to replicate old and decaying Kwakiutl poles. The slender thread of continuity, held by the last of the master carvers, was largely responsible for pulling Northwest Coast Indian art back from the brink of extinction. Mungo Martin continued this work at the British Columbia Provincial Museum in Victoria, working with two other Southern Kwakiutl carvers, Henry Hunt and his young son Tony, both of whom went on to become leading carvers. Because there were no experienced carvers from other cultures, they replicated Tsimshian and Haida poles as well.

Another significant name in the revival of the art is that of Bill Reid, Haida artist and jeweller, who with Doug Cranmer, a Kwakiutl carver from Alert Bay, undertook the massive project of recreating part of a Haida village for the Museum of Anthropology. Although a late starter, Bill Reid had diligently studied early Haida works of art and created superb pieces in silver, gold, argillite and wood, as well as high-quality silk-screen prints, providing a strong impetus to the revival of Northwest Coast Indian art. Adding to that stimulus, Haida artist, jeweller and carver Robert Davidson (an early apprentice of Reid's) brought back and revitalized many aspects of the early traditions of his people, and in 1968 he raised the first totem pole on the Queen Charlotte Islands in the twentieth century. The event, with its accompanying feast and ceremonies, aroused a new pride in the Haida nation.

Other young artists, notably Joe David of the Nuu-chah-nulth, Norman Tait of the Nishga (a division of the Tsimshian) and Nathan Jackson of the Tlingit, studied the early masterpieces of their forebears to resurrect the art styles of their particular cultures. All of them carved totem poles.

In 1951 when the ill-conceived law banning the potlatch was finally repealed after a long struggle, potlatching came into its own again, especially to mark major events such as the raising of a totem pole. Native elders reached back into their childhood memories to provide the new generation with information on ceremonies, crest use, rights and privileges, legends, regalia, songs, dances and other aspects of their traditions.

From the 1960s onward, awareness and appreciation of Northwest Coast art and its traditions grew steadily among non-natives, as did a renewed sense of self-identity and pride among the native people themselves.

A photograph taken in 1983 shows an old pole at Skedans on the Queen Charlotte Islands tilting back with age, yet it could remain standing for many more years.
PHOTOGRAPH BY HILARY STEWART

On the Upper Skeena River, in the replica Gitksan village of 'Ksan built in 1970, a school of art was established for teaching Northwest Coast Indian design, carving, jewellery and print making. Out of it grew an art style that, while reflecting the traditions of the Gitksan, made use of imaginative innovation. Many good artists and carvers had their start at the school.

A growing awareness of and interest in the sophisticated art form of the Northwest Coast Indian people has led to an expanding market in well crafted items made by native artisans. Quality gift shops and art galleries offer gold and silver jewellery, argillite carvings, drums, basketry, exquisitely carved and inlaid masks and headdresses, various ceremonial regalia—and many other items, including such contemporary works as silk-screen prints, carved plaques and bronze castings. And totem poles.

Now, more and more totem poles are being carved and raised with varying degrees of ceremony, and so strong has interest become in this specialized art that perhaps the majority of poles are commissioned for nontraditional purposes. Museums, corporations, governments, education centres, gift shops and private collectors often commission carvers to create new poles, several of which have gone to eastern Canada, the United States (other than Alaska), Mexico, England, Denmark, West Germany, Argentina, China, Japan and Australia.

The rekindled fires of Northwest Coast Indian culture burn brightly. Several villages have been or are involved in programs to replicate their old poles or to add new ones. So long as there are old growth forests to supply the cedar logs, totem poles will continue to be raised, radiating the power of the legendary and crest figures, telling of the people's pride in their past and of the strength of their culture, now and in the future.

TYPES OF TOTEM POLES

A variety of six different types of totem poles served different functions in the nineteenth-century villages of the coast, but not all tribal groups had all of them.

Traditionally, the Coast Salish were not totem pole carvers, though they did have large cedar planks, carved with high-relief figures of humans and animals, on the walls of their ceremonial dance houses. They also had house posts and grave figures carved in human form, but these are not really regarded as totem poles.

The Nuu-chah-nulth and Kwakiutl people set up a *welcome pole* near the village beach. This single, larger-than-life human figure, with arms outstretched, stood near the beach to welcome visitors arriving for a feast or potlatch. Both these tribal groups also integrated pairs of *house posts* inside the houses of high-ranking chiefs. Carved with the emblems of family histories, a pair of these poles stood at the back of the house to support the two main roof beams. Occasionally the posts at the opposite end, near the doorway, also carried carvings. Tlingit houses had frames similar to those of Kwakiutl houses, with twin main beams supported by four posts; carved house posts (separate from the actual structural posts) were often set in front of the pair of posts at the rear or in front of all four posts. Inside six-beam Haida houses, which had different frames, a single, massive house post, carved with family crests, stood at the rear of the house and supported one end of the ridge beam.

The *house frontal pole* of the Haida, Tsimshian, Kwakiutl and Tlingit stood up against the outside front of the house, with the doorway to one side of the pole. The pole carried the histories and crests of the family within, proclaiming their identity, worth and social standing. Such a pole was carved from a log split in half vertically, with the back hollowed out. This lessened the weight of the pole to make it easier to raise, removed any rot from the core of the log to prevent further rotting and allowed the pole to stand flush against the house front.

A similar pole, but with an oval entrance cut through the base, is termed a *house portal pole*. This special entrance was used on ceremonial occasions and gave particular significance to the guests and the processional entry into the house.

The *memorial pole*, found in Haida, Tlingit, Tsimshian and Kwakiutl villages,

Probably a good hundred years old, this mortuary pole at Skedans lies fallen amid forest growth in 1984, the victim of a windstorm. PHOTOGRAPH BY HILARY STEWART

stood before the house but was not attached to it. This pole could consist of a single crest at the base and/or top, or it could be elaborately carved along its full length. Raised about a year after the death of a chief, the memorial pole displayed crests and figures that depicted special achievements or events in the deceased's life. The succeeding chief gave the memorial potlatch, which also served as validation of his new position. The time span of at least a year was necessary to give the host family time to prepare and accumulate the gifts and food for the potlatch.

Another distinctive type of pole, found only among the Haida and Tlingit, rarely among the Tsimshian, was the *mortuary pole* for those of high rank. Generally carved with crests of the deceased, the mortuary pole had a large cavity cut into the upper end. At death, the body was placed in an elaborately painted chest or box, which was then put in a mortuary house. A year later the remains were placed in a smaller, undecorated box and deposited in the cavity of the mortuary pole. Cedar boards, shaped to resemble a large chest with lid and base, covered the open cavity at the front. Termed a frontal board, it was usually painted and sometimes carved with the main crest of the deceased. Additional planks covered the open top, with rocks placed on top to secure them against the wind. To allow maximum space for the box, the log of the mortuary pole was inverted, providing greater width at the top.

Among the Tlingit, a high-ranking person's body was cremated. In early times, the ashes were put in a box set on top of a plain pole. In later times, a carved crest figure, placed horizontally, replaced the box; and the ashes, in a small container, were placed in a niche at the back of the pole. There might also be a second niche for the ashes of a close family member. Sometimes the pole also carried carvings.

There is yet another category of pole, but examples of this type exist only in museums. It is the *shame pole*. This was carved for a chief who wished to ridicule or shame another—often his rival. Some misdeed, a long-standing unpaid debt or other incident worthy of scorn or ridicule, was publicly proclaimed by raising such a pole, which usually represented the person in question in some unflattering attitude. When restitution was made, the carving came down.

Contemporary times have brought a new category of totem pole into being— the commercial pole. These are commissioned from sources outside the culture, such as governments, corporations, institutions or private individuals. Generally the art and carving follow tradition, and such poles are often raised with ceremony, but their significance takes on a new role. Nonfunctional poles in untraditional places can be a strong reminder of the country's first nations and their highly developed skills in design and sculpture.

The function of totem poles varied somewhat among the different peoples, but overall they were historical monuments, or documents, of great meaning and value to the cultures that carved them. They displayed a people's origins and lineages, their supernatural experiences, their exploits and achievements, and their successes, acquisitions and territories. These recorded histories gave the people cultural identity, and proclaimed their wealth and status in the village and within their tribal group. Many poles, old and new, still serve the same purpose.

CARVING AND RAISING POLES

Almost without exception, totem poles were, and are, carved from the trunk of western red cedar (*Thuja plicata*). It took a person of knowledge to find and choose the right tree—one straight of grain, without convolutions, with a minimum of knots and preferably as close to the sea or a river as possible for ease of transport. Before bringing down the tree, the faller ritually addressed the spirit of the tree in prayer, asking it to fall in the right direction and for the wood not to split.

In early times there were several different ways of felling a tree: by controlled burning at its base, by placing red-hot rocks in a deeply chiselled cavity in the trunk, or by splitting out the wood from between two grooves circling the trunk. Once felled, the top section of the tree carrying the branches was removed by burning through it with red-hot rocks. The log was then skidded down to water and towed by canoe back to the village. Slaves, supervised by a specialist, carried out all the preparation work. In contemporary times, the tree is felled by chainsaw. Sometimes, especially if a very large log is required, it is chosen from a

The adze and the curved knife, in varying sizes, are two of the carver's most used tools. PHOTOGRAPH BY HILARY STEWART

The skilled hands of Robert Davidson carefully wield a specialized tool to shape the distinctive lines of a Haida pole at Skidegate, 1977. PHOTOGRAPH BY HILARY STEWART

boom of logs felled by a logging company and delivered to the carving site by truck.

With the log lying horizontally, the carver and his assistants, often apprentices, first stripped off the bark and then adzed away all the sapwood. Any damaged wood, large knots or other defective areas were cut out and replaced with sections of good wood, which were pegged in place.

A wealthy chief who wanted to raise a memorial pole, for instance, would commission an artist-carver with a good reputation, perhaps from another village. The chief told him what crests and other figures he wanted on the pole, and in what order, but the design and representation were up to the carver. He drew in the design with charcoal. After adzing, chiselling and splitting away the wood to give form to the figures, he brought out the final shaping and detailing with curved knives and incising tools. Elements such as outstretched wings, sun rays, dorsal fins, large beaks or anything extending out from the girth of the log required separately carved pieces to be added and joined by mortise and tenon or by pegging.

The finished carving then had paint applied (though not always); the areas painted and the choice of colour depended on the tradition of the area. Prior to European contact, pigments were made from grinding various minerals and mixing the powder with a binding agent, such as the glutinous part of salmon eggs. When commercial paints became available, these were readily used instead, and in fact broadened the palette of the painter.

If the making of the totem pole took place close to the village, a screen of brushwood or matting kept the work in progress hidden from view, so that no one should see the pole until the time came for raising it.

Raising a pole, especially a large one, required a great deal of preparation and skill. Many people helped to dig a hole before the pole was ceremonially carried to the site. It took perhaps a hundred or more men to carry the pole, which lay on crossbars supported on the carriers' shoulders. The uncarved base of the pole went into the hole, while the upper part leaned out at an angle, resting on supports. Under an expert's direction, many people hauled on strong ropes made from twisted cedar withes (or ship's rope acquired in trade) to raise the cedar column. Others pushed it up from beneath, using long poles, while still others took the tension on two more ropes to prevent the carved log from swaying to either side. The pole was raised in stages, resting on a log crutch between each stage. Drumming, singing and dancing punctuated the stages until the pole was standing vertically.

The hole in the ground around the base of the pole was filled in with rocks and dirt, with men tossing in boulders as large as they could carry. These rocks contributed to good drainage, which helped prevent rotting; their mass also kept the pole from falling long after it began to lean.

Different tribal groups had varying traditions for the pole-raising ceremonies: a popular Haida one was for the carver to dance with his tools tied around his person. Among all groups, the owner of the pole explained in detail the stories and meaning behind all the carved figures, and those assembled to witness the event were expected to remember what they saw and heard. A particularly fine pole called for praise, criticism and comparison, enhancing the status of the owner and the reputation of the carver.

Feasting and potlatching followed in celebration, as one more carved monument stood tall and splendid against the sky, changing the village skyline and adding prestige and status to the host family.

As with so many significant possessions of the Northwest Coast culture—houses, canoes and feast bowls, for example—totem poles had, and still have, names. The name may refer to a legend depicted on the pole, to the owner, or to the person for whom a memorial pole was raised.

The height of poles varies considerably, with the tallest (in the nineteenth century) being up to 18 m (60 feet). Modern pole-raising equipment has enabled this limit to be extended considerably; a pole of 30 m (100 feet) stands in Vancouver, another of nearly 39 m (127 feet) towers on a hill in Victoria, and in Kake, Alaska, a tremendously tall pole rises over 45 m (150 feet). In the village of Alert Bay, the world's tallest totem pole soars an astounding 52 m (173 feet) into the sky. (Its very height, however, has made it impracticable to include in this book, since reducing the drawing to fit the page would diminish the crests beyond recognition.)

Over time, and with wind and weather, an old pole may begin to tilt, then lean, and eventually fall. A fallen pole is never raised again because it would be too costly to give another potlatch and to pay those who help to raise the pole. In early times, a leaning pole that threatened a house or pathway might have been propped up, but once a pole fell, it was left to return to the earth. Nowadays, with renewed appreciation of the early cedar monuments, a metal support or brace may be added to help keep the pole upright.

The longevity of the pole depends on the environment, and whether the pole has been set into the ground or, as often happens now, set in a cement base above ground. Constant dampness hastens insect and fungus damage, and also encour-

Wood chips carpet the floor of a disused warehouse in Vancouver in 1982, as warmly dressed carvers work through the winter to finish Norman Tait's 16.7-m (55-foot) totem pole, Big Beaver, now in front of the Field Museum in Chicago. PHOTOGRAPH BY HILARY STEWART

This Haida house frontal pole, carved by Bill Reid, had a Dogfish spine and Whale dorsal fin added before being raised in Skidegate, 1978. PHOTOGRAPH BY HILARY STEWART

The traditional rigging used by Gitksan people to raise a free-standing pole. PHOTOGRAPH BY HILARY STEWART

A spruce seedling, photographed in 1981 growing in a crevice in a pole at Cumshewa on the Queen Charlotte Islands, has sent its root down through a crack in the wood and split the pole asunder. PHOTOGRAPH BY HILARY STEWART

Haida dignitaries in ceremonial attire during pole-raising ceremonies at Skidegate, 1978. PHOTOGRAPHY BY HILARY

ages plant growth. For example, a conifer seedling, especially spruce in the north, will send its root down through an existing crack in the wood; the root eventually grows so thick that it will split the pole in two.

Some poles last sixty to eighty years, and a few have stood for longer, though the carving has deteriorated considerably. Often the side of the pole facing the prevailing winds and rain may be quite rotted, while the lee side is still in a good state of preservation. This is quite noticeable at Ninstints and Skedans in the Queen Charlotte Islands, where some standing poles are more than a hundred years old. Cracks and splits in totem poles are natural for an organic material such as wood, and should not be seen as a disfigurement or flaw in the carving.

Bringing old poles indoors will preserve them indefinitely, but there is something special about a pole that stands outdoors, perhaps facing river or sea, backed by mountain or forest. Or even on a city street.

A contemporary pole raising may have many of the elements of its early traditions, such as the speeches, singing, drumming and providing food for all. It may also include a full-blown potlatch that involves the feeding of many hundreds of people at a lavish sit-down dinner featuring many traditional native foods.

To haul on the ropes that raise a bright new pole, to witness, to feast, to hear speeches in a language still preserved, to receive gifts, to watch masked dancers while smoke from the central fire billows up and out through the smoke hole, is to be a part of that pole's history. It is also a privilege.

PART 2 LOOKING AT TOTEM POLES

CARVED FIGURES

Although artistically unique and visually splendid, totem poles may at first appear to be bewildering because of their maze of complex imagery. It is important to remember that the pole shape dictates that (with a few exceptions) all the figures be portrayed vertically. Humans and humanlike beings may be carved standing fully upright, but more often they are depicted in a crouched position, with knees either bent or doubled up, and with arms flexed. Four-legged animals, especially Bear and Beaver, are shown in similar attitudes. Birds are usually shown as perched, with wings at their sides or outstretched; legs have clawed feet, and beaks extend out horizontally or are tucked downward against the chest.

The bodies of almost all creatures face the front, but some are portrayed as if seen from above, with the head either uppermost or downward on the pole. Figures best suited to this are Whale, Dogfish, Salmon, Frog and Wolf.

Small, secondary creatures may be shown as complete, or with head and forearms (or forelegs) emerging from behind some other figure. There may also be overlapping or interlocking of various beings, which makes it more difficult to unscramble the different figures, but careful examination of the carving will help identification.

A pole should be "read" from the top down. The top figure on a pole, perhaps Raven, Eagle or Thunderbird, may identify the owner through his crest. Contrary to popular belief, the "top man on the totem pole" is not the highest ranking or the most important—in fact, he carries the least significance. It is the largest figure, generally the one at the base of the pole, which is the most prominent in the story, with secondary smaller figures having less importance. Quite small creatures serve to fill in areas such as ears, the space on the chest or between the thighs. Their presence carries some meaning, but on old or replica poles the significance has been lost to antiquity. Interpretation of some of the very old poles is impossible if no documentation exists. At best the figures portrayed can be identified, but not the context.

CRESTS

There is Sea Bear, the Cannibal-Bird Hokw-hokw and the Two-headed Sea Serpent Sisiutl. There is Flying-Frog, One-Horned Mountain Goat and Five-Finned Killer Whale. There is Split-Person, Fog-Woman, Running-Backwards and a whole host of other mythical supernatural beings that have become the crests of the various cultures of the Northwest Coast peoples.

Singly, or multiply with one above other, these images embellish the carved wooden monuments to proclaim a people's beginnings, history and lineage. The figures record the past, display it in the present, and preserve it for the future.

Many of the crests have their origins in the ancient myth time before the world was as it is now, a time when humans and animals were not separate and distinct, when they could transform easily from one to another and frequently did. A family comes to own its "origin" crest through an early ancestor who had a memorable adventure or encounter with a supernatural creature. This adventure often entailed the ancestor's overcoming and killing the creature, or the creature becoming human to establish the lineage. The ancestor and all his descendants have the right to use that creature's likeness on totem poles, house fronts, interior screens, boxes, feast dishes, ceremonial regalia and any other property. If the ancestor received a song and a dance at the time of the encounter, his descendants inherit the right to perform that dance wearing a mask in the likeness of the creature, and to sing that song; no one else has the right to that song or that dance.

However, a crest could also be acquired through marriage, obtained by the conquest of an enemy, traded, given in compensation for special services, or appropriated at the extinction of a family. Outstanding episodes of family history, migrations and settlement, war adventures, resource ownership, or special visions could generate new crests, which would be validated by a potlatch.

As well as birds, fish, mammals and supernatural beings, there were crests such as insects, plants, celestial bodies and natural phenomena: Mosquito, Woodworm, Starfish, Fireweed, Fern, Sun, Moon, Stars, Rainbow and Sundog are some of these. The rich array of crests on carved poles does not portray the ordinary creatures of nature, but spiritual, supernatural beings. To clarify the difference, their names, when written, are capitalized in this book. In addition to displaying individual crest figures, a pole may depict some of the additional characters of an encounter story, together with objects that are a part of the story. These may be a cave, a glacier, a spear, a string of fish, a talking stick, a box, a canoe, twin cubs, a child and so on.

The list of crest figures to be found on poles is quite lengthy and includes some rather cryptic beings as well as supernatural personifications. However, the following, though brief, covers most of the carvings illustrated in this book, and others are pointed out as they appear.

Mythical Beings

THUNDERBIRD: For many people, Thunderbird is the very essence of a totem pole. Thunderbird, a huge and powerful creature, is the most powerful of all spirits, and could be taken as a crest only by very high-ranking and powerful chiefs. All the coastal peoples include Thunderbird in one form or another in their ancient lore and attribute various powers to this supernatural bird. He is known to swoop down from the sky to capture a surfacing whale in his huge talons, then to fly off to the mountains to eat the sea mammal. Thunder rolls from the great bird's wing beat, and lightning flashes from its blinking eyes.

Thunderbird has a beak like that of Eagle or Hawk, but also has curled appendages (sometimes referred to as horns) on its head; these may represent tufts of curled feathers.

Depictions of this mighty bird range from subtle to exuberant: Kwakiutl carvers most often and most dramatically depict it with outstretched or uplifted multifeathered wings atop many a pole.

THUNDERBIRD

KOLUS, KULUS, OR QUOLUS: Kolus, the younger brother of Thunderbird, also has tufts on its head, but instead of curling they are straight and horizontal. Kolus is described in myth as being covered with dazzling white down that causes him to become greatly overheated. To overcome this, he can remove his coat of down, revealing his human image. Like his older brother, Kolus is endowed with great strength. He is credited with lifting into place huge house beams too heavy for humans to raise and with moving house frames into position.

HOKW-HOKW, HOK-HOK, OR HUXW-HUXW: The very long, straight beak is that of Hokw-hokw, a fabulous bird-monster. He is one of three servants in the cannibal spirit Bakbakwalanuksiwe's great house in the sky, at the north end of the

KOLUS

35

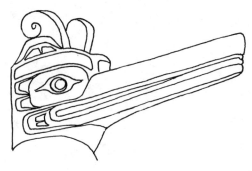

HOKW-HOKW

world. Under control of the cannibal spirit, a series of extraordinary mythical beings play a vital role in the ceremonies initiating a novice into the Hamatsa dancing society of the Kwakiutl. During the complex rituals, dancers wear the appropriate masks, fringed with shredded cedar bark, to dramatically portray these creatures.

Hokw-hokw, with his extraordinary long, chisel-shaped beak, cracks open the skulls of men and devours their brains. During the dance of Hokw-hokw, the mask's beak is manipulated by the dancer to repeatedly open and snap shut, making a loud clacking sound.

As a totem pole crest, this monstrous cannibal-bird is depicted as eaglelike, but with large flaring nostrils on its long slender beak, which is a separate attachment on the pole.

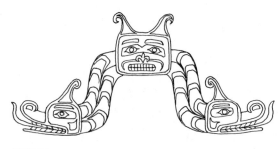

SISIUTL

SISIUTL, SISIOOHL, OR SISIYUTL: A dramatic, supernatural creature often depicted by Kwakiutl carvers and artists is Sisiutl, the scaly sea serpent with the power to bring both good and evil. Sisiutl can change itself into various forms, including a self-propelled canoe—which the owner must feed with seals. Touching the serpent, or even looking at it, or a glare from it, can cause death, and yet it is a source of magical powers. It can bring wealth and, when painted over a doorway, it serves as guardian to the house.

The two-headed sea serpent is closely associated with war and strength, and with death and revival; its blood rubbed on a warrior made him invulnerable, and wearing a head band or belt in the image of Sisiutl afforded a warrior protection from harm.

Flakes of shiny mica found on beaches and elsewhere were thought to be the discarded scales from this awesome sea serpent's body.

Carved or painted, Sisiutl is depicted with a profile head, teeth, and a large curled tongue at each end of its serpentine form; in the centre is a human head. Fins run along its back, and curled appendages, or "horns," rise from all three heads. The body is painted to represent scales. Sisiutl may be carved horizontally, or formed into a U shape, or coiled into a circle.

DZOONOKWA, DZONOQUA, DZUNUKWA, OR TSONOQOA: A fearsome giantess of the dark forest, this not-quite-human female is also known as Wild Woman of the Woods and Property Woman. She is often the subject of prints, paintings, masks and other carvings, including totem poles, where she is always painted in black, with pendulant breasts, heavy eyebrows, deep-set eye sockets with half-closed eyes—and pursed lips to indicate her cry of "Ooh-ooh, ooh-ooh."

By character Dzoonokwa is stupid, clumsy and sleepy—hence the slit or crescent eyes. She captures children who are crying or who venture alone into the forest, carrying them away in a basket on her back to devour them.

The house of this awesome giantess is filled with wonderful treasures such as boxes of food, coppers, canoes and more. Through special encounters with Dzoonokwa, a person could acquire some of this wealth and supernatural power.

Many non-native people also know of this shaggy, forest-dwelling giant: in Canada they refer to her (and him) as Sasquatch, and in the United States as Bigfoot.

DZOONOKWA

WATCHMEN: Elaborately carved Haida house frontal poles often carry at the top one to four (generally three) small, crouched human figures, wearing high-crowned hats. Known as Watchmen, they have supernatural powers, and from their lofty position atop the pole, they look out in several directions to keep watch over the village and out to sea. They protect those within the dwelling by warning the chief of the house of any approaching danger, alerting him to canoes arriving or anything else he should know. The high-crowned hats worn by the Watchmen symbolize the status of the chief whose house they guard.

WATCHMAN

Land-Sea Mammals

Often, creatures of the supernatural world include land mammals with marine associations and physical attributes. Supernatural beings in touch with both worlds, they can move freely from one to the other. Thus, a totem pole may have a depiction of Sea Bear, Sea Wolf, Sea Grizzly or a legendary sea monster of some type. Generally, but not always, such a creature may be portrayed both with its land animal characteristics and with fins, flippers or a fluked tail.

Other Beings

Several guidelines can help to identify other beings, but, as with most rules, there are always exceptions. The birds are depicted with similar bodies, but their heads have differing characteristics or symbols. All the birds are generally shown with

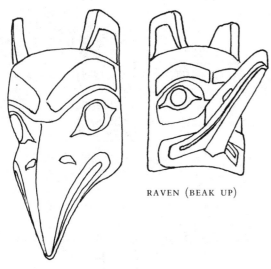

RAVEN (BEAK UP)

RAVEN (BEAK DOWN)

EAGLE

eyebrows and ears atop their heads, as are the animals. Raven has a straight (but not overly long) beak, Eagle has a short beak downturned at the tip, while Hawk (or Mountain Hawk) has a beak that is downturned and recurved inward.

Bear is distinguished by prominent ears, round or flared nostrils, and generally a menacing display of teeth that includes pointed canines. This very humanlike animal is usually shown sitting upright in a human stance, with large clawed paws on all four legs.

Beaver is readily identified by two large incisor teeth, round nostrils and a cross-hatched tail that generally has a human face where the tail joins the body. Beaver often is shown holding a chewing stick in its front paws.

Wolf can be similar to Bear, except that it is more slender, has tall ears, a much longer snout and a lot of teeth. The tail may be bushy and curled, or straight and black-tipped, depending on the cultural tradition.

Mainly seen on northern poles, though not very often, Mountain Goat has hoofed feet and two slender curved horns. Also found frequently in the north is Frog, who displays a wide mouth with no teeth. It has no ears, but it does have large round eyes and clawlike representations of toes.

One of the most often depicted crests is Whale. Killer Whale carries a long dorsal fin and short pectoral fins, whereas Humpback or Grey Whale is distinguished by a short dorsal fin and long slender pectorals. As well, they are shown with painted spots on their backs—perhaps representing the large barnacles found on the backs of these sea mammals. All Whales have rounded snouts, large mouths, symmetrical tail flukes and blowholes that often appear as human faces. Carved on a pole, the tail may be flat or curved back over the creature's back.

Fish generally take their natural shape, with Bullhead having a very large head and Sculpin having many spines. Frequently seen on Haida poles is Dogfish (or Shark), unmistakable with its high, domed forehead, gill slits and pointed teeth in a large downturned mouth, which may have a labret in the lower lip. Asymmetrical tail flukes identify this large fish, which may also have small dorsal fins and spines.

Mosquito may take a humanlike form, or have several legs, but is recognizable by its long, narrow proboscis.

A human face, carved or painted on a bird or mammal, may represent its duality, and sometimes the transformation from one to the other is portrayed by the depiction of body parts from both, on the same figure.

Sun is easily recognized by the rays around its circular face, while Moon has a round rim but no rays.

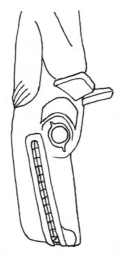

HAWK
(OR MOUNTAIN HAWK)

BEAR

BEAVER

WOLF

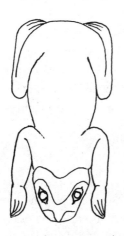

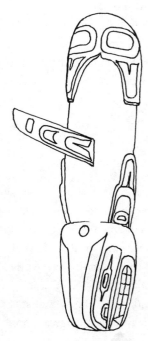

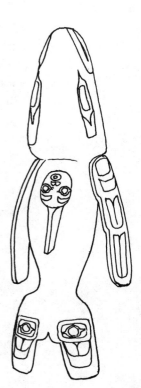

FROG (HEAD DOWN)

KILLER WHALE

DOGFISH (OR SHARK)

HUMPBACK (OR GREY) WHALE

39

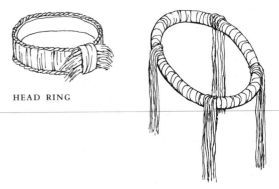

HIGH-CROWNED OR RINGED HAT

HEAD RING

NECK RING

The High-Crowned or Ringed Hat

The tall hat with several rings around the high crown, seen on northern poles, is a representation of the hats worn by high-ranking Haida and Tlingit people. Finely woven of split spruce roots, the wide-brimmed hats have several woven cylinders topping the crown. These are called *skils*. It is popularly thought that the number of cylinders, or rings, represents the number of potlatches given by the owner, giving rise to the term "potlatch rings" or "potlatch cylinders." This concept may have originated with the number of times the crest hat had been displayed and revalidated as a crest at potlatches.

Another theory is that a specific number of rings or cylinders was, in itself, a crest. This seems quite probable, since some of these hats, painted with family crests, were crests themselves. Certainly, the high-crowned or ringed hat points to chiefly status and high rank, and poles that include these hats symbolize the status of the chiefs on whose poles they are carved.

Occasionally, a plain column of such rings was carved on a pole, in association with a figure, human or animal; or a whole section of a pole was carved to represent the stacked cylinders.

The Head Ring and Neck Ring

Made of inner cedar bark, the head ring was worn by a person taking part in certain ceremonies, dances or rituals. The bark, shredded and dyed red, was woven or braided or otherwise formed into a crownlike ring for the head, and sometimes it was decorated with fur and/or abalone shell.

Similarly, the neck ring, also made of inner cedar bark, was worn at special functions, hung around the neck or at times worn across one shoulder. The neck ring varied in size, and often had sections of long fringes of cedar bark twine hanging from it. Head and neck rings are still worn in present-day ceremonies.

The Copper

The copper, which derives its English name from the metal of its manufacture, is an item that represents great wealth and prestige among the native people of northern Vancouver Island and northward.

The copper's characteristic shape has a flared upper half, which carries a painted design; it also has ridges hammered into a T shape. With an average height of about 70 cm (28 inches), excluding miniatures, coppers of the past were made from sheet copper—often of the type used for sheathing the wooden hulls of sailing ships—and were acquired in trade.

The metal itself symbolized wealth and high rank. Northern chiefs proclaimed their rank and lineage by displaying many large coppers at a potlatch. Each copper had a name and a history, and represented a specific value.

Among the Kwakiutl, a chief could take revenge on anyone who had insulted him or his family by publicly and ceremonially breaking off a section of a copper and presenting it to the offender. A copper could be broken several times and repaired, adding to its history and value. Melting a copper in a fire or throwing it into the sea was a conspicuous gesture of disregard for one's enormous wealth. Coppers of great value could be used towards purchasing slaves, a stand of fine cedars, hunting lands, or other food resources or property.

One or more coppers might be nailed to a mortuary or memorial pole, or be depicted on a pole to proclaim a person's rank and status.

COPPER

The Labret

On the Northwest Coast, the labret was an ornament worn by women in a perforation through the lower lip. In the north, labrets were oval in shape, generally made of wood or stone, sometimes inlaid with small flat pieces of shell or bone. The wearing of a labret signified high rank.

Labrets of a different style have only been found archaeologically in southern coast areas, indicating that the practice fell out of use there long before European contact. Eighteenth-century explorers and traders to the north coast, however, commented on this ornament, and nineteenth-century photographers recorded women wearing the labret.

Although no longer worn, labrets are sometimes depicted on masks, totem poles and other carvings of high-ranking women.

LABRET

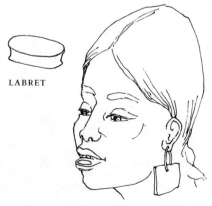

WOMAN WEARING LABRET

41

Talking Stick or Speaker's Staff

When giving a speech at a formal gathering, a chief holds in his right hand a long wooden staff that resembles a miniature totem pole. It may have a single crest at the top, or be fully carved all the way down the shaft. The talking stick represents the chief's authority to speak, and often he will thump it on the floor or against the ground, or manipulate it in other ways, to emphasize his words or make a point. This ceremonial item is still used today by high-ranking speakers, and contemporary carvers sometimes include it on poles.

THE DEPICTION OF LEGENDS

The use of the word "legend" does not imply that a story is fictional. A legend is, to quote *Webster's Dictionary*: "a story coming down from the past, especially one handed down from early times by tradition, and popularly regarded as history"—and, in *Collins' Dictionary*: "a marvellous story of ancient times, a traditional tale."

Certain legends repeatedly appear in carved form on totem poles, and may be readily recognized by the depiction of figures central to the story. While details of most stories vary from one coastal culture to another—even from one village to another—the basics remain constant.

Some aspects of these legends may seem mystifying in today's world, but that does not negate their reality to a people whose culture encompassed a spiritual and cosmic understanding of their environment. Traditional knowledge lies behind these marvellous stories handed down from early times, and belief in them was as closely held as those of any other deeply rooted culture or religion.

Nanasimget and the Whale

A long and complex Haida story is that of Nanasimget, a young man who married a wealthy and very beautiful woman. As he set out to go seal hunting one day, his grandmother pointed out a white sea otter among the kelp. After a long hunt he managed to spear it beneath the tail so the pelt would be unmarked and perfect. In skinning it, the old woman got a spot of blood on the fur; the wife offered to clean it in a tide pool, but she slipped on a rock and the otter pelt fell into the sea.

The young woman went in after the skin; just as she touched it, a Whale rose up from beneath, lifting her out of the water, then swam off across the sea while she desperately hung onto his dorsal fin. Nanasimget gave chase in his canoe, but the Whale dove and did not surface again.

After preparing himself ceremonially, Nanasimget returned to the place where the Whale and his wife had descended, and dove into the sea. On the sea bed he found a trail and followed it. After encounters with three geese, a heron and a watchman with wooden legs, he was told that his wife was to marry the Whale as soon as a dorsal fin had been made for her.

In a bid to rescue his wife, Nanasimget conspired with the slave who was making the fin. Thus, when the slave entered the Whale's house with a container of water for steaming the fin, he spilled it on the fire. With clouds of steam filling the house, Nanasimget dashed in to where the slave had told him his wife was sitting, grabbed her, and ran out again. Together, they raced along the trail to the kelp stem to which his canoe was tied, climbed up it into the canoe, and paddled back to the village, foiling the Whale's attempts to pursue them.

Many a carved pole records this narrative by depicting Whale, with a woman on his back or clinging to his fin, and Nanasimget, who gave chase. Other cultural groups have variations of this legend of a Whale abducting a woman.

How Raven Stole the Sun

Perhaps the best-known legend on the Northwest Coast, and the one with the most variations, tells how Raven the trickster stole the Sun—as well as the Moon and the Stars—and brought daylight to the world. Details of the story may change considerably from one cultural area to another or from one village to another, but the basic components usually remain fairly constant.

There was a time when all the world was in darkness because a greedy chief kept the Sun, the Moon and the Stars in three wooden boxes in his house. He would occasionally lift the lid and let the light spill out for a short while, but he jealously guarded these treasured possessions.

Hearing about the boxes, Raven was determined to bring daylight to the world, but since no one was allowed to touch the boxes, the wily bird devised a cunning plan. Knowing that the chief's daughter went to the stream for water every day, Raven transformed himself into a hemlock needle and floated down the stream. When the young woman filled her box with fresh, cool water, he slid unnoticed into the box and was carried to the house.

The chief's daughter drank some of the water, swallowed the hemlock needle, and as a result became pregnant. Eventually she gave birth to a dark, beady eyed child, who grew at an astounding rate. He also cried a lot, mostly for the box with the bright, shiny ball inside, but the chief refused to allow him to play with it. Daily the child wheedled and whined and cried even louder and longer, until the chief could stand it no more and allowed his grandson to play with the ball of light—just this once.

Seizing his long awaited opportunity, Raven quickly transformed himself back into bird form, picked up the ball in his beak, and in a flash of black feathers flew up and out through the smoke hole. Higher and higher and farther and farther he flew, spreading light all around the world for everyone to enjoy. Then he flung the shining globe into the sky, and there it remains—even to this day.

Carved or painted depictions of this story may show Raven, the chief, his daughter and the Sun, which sometimes appears as a face with rays emanating from it, sometimes as a disc. On occasion, the box that held the Sun is also included, but in its most minimal form the Sun may simply be shown as a ball or disc in Raven's beak.

The Bear Mother

One spring, a woman of high rank was helping to harvest the luscious red salmonberries when she accidentally slipped on a pile of Bear dung. With spilled berries and hurt dignity, she hurled insults at the one responsible. The Bear, feeding on salmonberries on the nearby bushes, overheard the tirade and kidnapped the woman, taking her back to his village.

Imprisoned in a small wooden structure with a barricaded door, the captive was alone and upset. Presently, tiny Mouse Woman appeared and said to her: "You must break your copper bracelet in half. After the Bears feed you, they will allow you out into the forest to empty your bowels, but they will be guarding you. Scrape out a hollow for the excrement, cover it over, and secretly drop the half bracelet on top. Do the same again the next day."

The woman did as Mouse Woman bade her. Now, when the Bear chief was informed that the woman's dung was in fact copper, he was very impressed and apologized for mistreating her. Her request to return home was denied, but eventually she was persuaded to marry the Bear chief's nephew. In time the woman gave birth to twin cubs and settled down, resigned to her new life.

Eventually, however, the woman's two brothers came with dogs to search for her, and not wanting a confrontation, the Bear father fled with his family to hide in a cave. But the search party pursued them until they discovered the family, and after a discussion, an agreement was made: the brothers could establish a Bear clan if they would not smoke the Bear out of his den, but instead kill him ceremonially and sing a special mourning song afterwards. And this they did.

The brothers returned home with their sister and her twin cubs, and took Bear for their crest. Soon after, the cubs went home to their own village; the mother remarried and had human children to further propagate the Bear clan, whose crest is seen on many poles.

Thus, whenever a bear was killed for its meat and its hide, the special mourning song was always sung.

CULTURAL ART STYLES

The different styles of design on totem poles among Northwest Coast peoples may at first look alike, but among the various cultural groups there are, in fact, distinct differences in style that can be determined by observation and comparison.

Early in the carving renaissance, some of the young, less experienced carvers and artists tended to be influenced by the art styles of the north, regardless of their cultural background. As a result, jewellery, silk-screen prints and carvings often had a similarity of style. But as their interest in their heritage deepened, many of the artists made a point of studying museum pieces to determine more closely the authentic styles representative of their own cultural groups. Today, experienced carvers tend to stay closely within the bounds of their own cultural carving traditions. Certainly there are innovations, but these usually fall within the appropriate cultural style.

The following is a brief guide to distinguishing the different styles of totem poles on the Northwest Coast, with particular reference to those illustrated in this book.

Coast Salish

Although the Coast Salish were accomplished carvers, they did not have totem poles. Many small pieces attest to their carving skill, as do large panels and house posts found in their early ceremonial dance houses, as well as elaborate grave figures. The Coast Salish style of large carving was in general quite realistic, with humans depicted in more or less correct proportion and natural attitudes. Faces were portrayed minimally and simply, without the carved contours found elsewhere, and little or no paint was applied. Animals, too, were shown realistically and fully carved in the round, emerging from the wooden plank background.

Nuu-chah-nulth (formerly Nootka or Westcoast)

In spite of a well-developed art tradition and carving ability, totem poles came late to the Nuu-chah-nulth people, probably because they did not have a formal crest system such as those to the north of them. Known for their carved house posts and for their welcome poles, the Nuu-chah-nulth did not erect poles depicting multiple figures until the twentieth century. Although few in number, these reflected the style of their traditional painted designs.

In creating new poles, contemporary carvers are incorporating the stylistic tradition found in the old graphic arts and applying it to three-dimensional form. This gives the present-day Nuu-chah-nulth poles a distinct appearance.

Not having clan emblems to portray, the artists carve humans, birds, animals and mythical creatures to depict not only legends of their people but also traditional activities and customs.

Human proportion is about one-quarter head to three-quarters body. The overall design is contained within the column of the log; occasionally, appendages are added. Flowing, curved shapes are characteristic, as are rounded U forms with parallel sides. Look for two split U forms, joined end to end to create a four-way split, somewhat resembling a four-pointed star. The northern style ovoid is almost nonexistent, but a round-cornered rectangle is used for eye sockets and elsewhere.

Eyes are not set back in the head to create high cheekbones or deep eye sockets, but face painting is often evident. This painting frequently crosses the carved planes rather than following them, as among the Kwakiutl. The paint colours used are mainly red, black and a light green or blue-green. Contemporary welcome figures, which are not painted, tend to follow the old style.

Several Nuu-chah-nulth artist-carvers have re-established many of the values and ceremonies of their culture, giving fresh impetus to the carving of canoes, rattles, masks and other ceremonial items—all in traditional style.

Kwakiutl

Although there are differences between the Northern and Southern Kwakiutl carving styles, the lack of Northern Kwakiutl pole carvers has resulted in all the poles illustrated in this volume being Southern Kwakiutl. These are carved in a style that dates from around the last decade of the nineteenth century.

Several characteristics distinguish these poles from those of other cultures. In general they are more exuberant and more embellished. The contour of the cylindrical log is likely to be deeply indented, and often there is asymmetry in the design. Perhaps the most common figure is that of Thunderbird, with widely outstretched wings. Body proportion is about one-third to two-thirds torso, with an equal ratio of humans and animals intermingled; figures are shown separately rather than interlocked and often holding a small figure. Projections include long beaks, wings, fins and sun rays.

Kwakiutl poles do not contain multiple figures that combine to depict a story; each figure is a crest, but many of these carry their own legend or context. Mythical figures such as Dzoonokwa, Sisiutl, Kolus and Hokw-hokw are unique to the Kwakiutl.

Free from formalism, these poles often show imagination and flair. Typically, Kwakiutl carvers created the world's two tallest totem poles, as well as the world's biggest in diameter. Often a broad range of colour is used—yellow, green, turquoise, brown and white, as well as the usual red and black. Many poles are entirely covered with paint, and most have elaborate and complex patterning. Eyes are small and rounded, often with two concentric circles set in deeply carved sockets with heavy brows. Multiple feathers are painted on a bird's outspread wings, tail, chest and legs. Sisiutl's body can be richly patterned with scales and a humanlike face, decorated with ovoids and U forms.

Kwakiutl poles tend to be tall and slender. The entire carving may be finished with the texture of fine adzing, a technique once considered essential to a carved pole.

Haida

Bold, elegant and monumental, good Haida poles are sophisticated masterpieces of design. The carved figures are mainly birds and animals—as well as supernatural creatures—which represent lineage crests or depict legends from which crests originated. The human form, not often portrayed, appears as diminutive, usually peeking from within, or between, the large ears of some creature, or lying on its chest, or crouched at the top as Watchmen.

Part of the monumental quality of Haida poles lies in the proportion of figures, with the head occupying half the total figure size. Adding to this massive impression is the device of interlocking or overlapping one figure with another, creating an almost unbroken, integrated column. Bilateral symmetry is almost a golden rule, and though the carving is often deep, the profile of the log is maintained.

The few appendages added, usually beaks and fins, are relatively short and are placed centrally. Eyes are huge and round, with outlined lids that are carved, set into fairly shallow ovoid eye sockets; eyebrows are heavy, and the ears of animals rise prominently. Arms and legs in the crouched position appear to be emerging out of the log rather than being superimposed on it. The overall design carries balance, symmetry, unity and boldness that sit well on the massive cedar trunks.

Paint is sparsely applied, sometimes not at all; black for eyebrows, eyes and lids, also any large ovoids and U forms, such as feathers—with red for nostrils, lips, tongues and split U forms. Blue is commonly used for eye sockets. Most of the wood is left in its natural colour, smoothly finished.

In keeping with the size of the huge, old-growth cedar trees of their homeland, the Queen Charlotte Islands, the Haida carvers create tall poles of considerable girth. Whether making replica or original poles, the Haida maintain the early traditional style of their skilled forefathers.

Gitksan, Nishga and 'Ksan (Tsimshian)

The Gitksan, who live on the Skeena River, and the Nishga, who live on the Nass River, once shared a similar style of totem pole carving. However, in the initial phase of the Gitanmaax School of Northwest Coast Indian art at 'Ksan, near Hazelton on the Skeena River, the carving instructors were Haida, or carvers working in the Haida style; as a result the now established art style of 'Ksan carries overtones of that period.

The Gitksan have many old poles (and replicas of old poles) dating from the nineteenth century, together with more recent poles that were carved especially for places such as commercial institutions, the 'Ksan cultural centre and the band office at Kispiox.

In general, Gitksan and Nishga poles depict both human and animal figures; the older poles more frequently depict humans with slender arms and legs that curve around the shape of the log. Head ratio is about one-third of the figure, and in some villages a row of several quite small human figures (a crest) forms an intricate band around the pole, separating one large figure from another. Eyes are round, but not as large as those on Haida poles, set in concave eye sockets that give way to prominent cheekbones; lips are not as thick as on Haida poles, and hands are often holding something. Poles tend to be tall and slender, sometimes with the top section uncarved; red and black paint is used sparingly, if at all.

The characteristics that differentiate Nishga poles from Gitksan ones are subtle:

A Nishga pole in Stanley Park, Vancouver.
PHOTOGRAPH BY HILARY STEWART

49

noses and cheeks are more rounded, as are foreheads and, interestingly, the eyes appear to be looking down rather than staring straight ahead. Generally, Gitksan and Nishga figures are all crests that represent stories documenting family histories, territories, rights and privileges. Although the Nishga carver represented in this book, Norman Tait, has chosen to fully illustrate legends on two of his poles, these are outside his village and do not belong to a Nishga family in the traditional manner. In his carving, he strives to define and maintain the old original style of his people.

Tlingit

The style of Tlingit poles falls within the general style of northern carving and design, but with some differences. The head ratio is closer to one-third of the total body length, arms and legs are more slender, and there is less interlocking of figures.

Depictions of humans and animals are about equal in number. Wings of birds (when added as appendages to the pole) are opened and vertical, unlike the widely outstretched horizontal wings of Kwakiutl bird figures.

The carved area often continues farther around the log, resulting in substantial carving interest on the sides of the pole. Paint is added to accentuate certain features: bodies of humans and animals are frequently painted solid red, and wings are often patterned with feather designs. Colours are mainly red, black and blue-green, though some contemporary poles have other colours and more painted areas.

Tlingit mortuary poles are distinctive, with a fully sculptured crest resting horizontally on the top of the log, which is also carved, sometimes partially.

Northern

The term "Northern" is used to define the art style of a carving or other design that is not clearly defined as being Haida, Tsimshian or Tlingit. Although the three nations have distinct characteristic art styles, they also share much in common, and at times their parameters can be blurred.

PART 3 TOTEM POLES

1 LOCATION: *Douglas border crossing*
CARVER: *Mungo Martin*
CULTURAL STYLE: *Haida*

This exceptionally fine Haida pole greets people who enter Canada via the Douglas border crossing from Blaine, Washington.

The badly decayed original of this pole was collected in 1954 from Skedans on the Queen Charlotte Islands. Leading families with close ties to the remote and long-abandoned village consented to the sale of the pole. This and other poles from various village sites were taken to the British Columbia Provincial Museum in Victoria for restoration and replication by the Kwakiutl master carver Mungo Martin.

In 1957 Haida artist Bill Reid, who had not yet attempted working on a large scale with wood, took a ten-day holiday from his job as an announcer with CBC Radio and joined Mungo to experience carving a totem pole. The elderly carver was working on the replica of the Skedans pole; pointing to a small human figure roughed in part way along the log, he said to Reid, "You carve there." Reid picked up a sharp carving knife and began working. Some time later, he asked, "Mungo, where are the Band-Aids?" and the old-time carver replied simply: "We don't use 'em," inferring that he never cut himself.

The original pole, a house portal pole, had an oval opening for a doorway and fronted a house at the easternmost end of Skedans village. Topped by three Watchmen, the figure below is probably Mountain Hawk (the Haida version of Thunderbird), who was actually a supernatural man wearing a feathered coat and had talons strong enough to catch whales. Notice the small Whale, head down, between the wings. The upside-down face on the bird's tail may represent its human form.

The figure below Mountain Hawk is that of a mythical animal, and the man in the high-crowned hat is probably the owner of the pole. At the base, Grizzly Bear guards the entrance to the house.

6 ft.
1.8 m

6 ft.
1.8 m

2 LOCATION: *Vancouver—Heritage Park on Musqueam Indian Reserve*
CARVER: *Stan Greene*
CULTURAL STYLE: *Coast Salish*

This carved figure—and the wood sculpture on the next page—are not in fact totem poles, which the Coast Salish never had. However, these two pieces are included so that all the major cultural groups and their styles of large woodcarving can be represented.

This single standing figure is a replica of the original house post from a ceremonial dance house in Musqueam, a native village with an ancient past on the Fraser River. A beam was once set into the slot at the top of the post. An 1898 photo shows the original post still standing, though the house is gone.

The stylistic carving is typical of large Coast Salish sculpture, as are the flat face, the horizontal brow ridge and small eyes. The identity of the man depicted is not known, but he may have been the owner of the house or an ancestor.

After this house post and the house board on the next page were repaired and painted by members of the Musqueam Band, both pieces were purchased by the University of British Columbia's Graduating Class of 1927 and donated to the university's Museum of Anthropology.

The two carvings were displayed outdoors on the campus until increasing decay warranted their being brought indoors. The house post proved to be rotted beyond repair, but in 1986, under the direction of the Museum of Anthropology, the post was replicated by Stan Greene, a Coast Salish artist and carver from the Fraser Valley. He worked from early photographs and took measurements of the fragments of the original in storage. The new carving was displayed at Vancouver's Expo 86. After the fair, the village of Musqueam acquired the post.

During building excavations in the village, early burial boxes with human remains had been discovered. These were left undisturbed, but skeletal remains uncovered during an archaeological excavation (the St. Mungo site) on the banks of the Fraser River, upstream from Musqueam, were reburied alongside the boxes. This plot of land became Heritage Park; now the recarved figure of the old house post stands there as a monument to the deceased and as a link between past and present.

3 LOCATION: *Vancouver—Totem Park Residences, 2525 West Mall, University of British Columbia*
CARVER: *Simon Charlie*
CULTURAL STYLE: *Coast Salish*

The house post on the facing page has long been associated with this house board, which is carved in high relief. In situ, the board would have been attached to a vertical post inside a house, along with other such boards.

Harlan I. Smith of the anthropology division of the National Museum in Ottawa saw and photographed the two carvings in 1898. Around 1923 Smith spoke with a Colonel Brown, who asked what was to be done with the Musqueam "poles," which he had found lying on the ground while out hiking. Smith is credited with saying that if the poles were still there, they would be very valuable. He had tried to acquire them twenty-five years before, for a museum in New York, but the Department of Indian Affairs had refused permission for them to be removed. He added that they were the only surviving specimens of their kind for the Coast Salish.

In 1963 the University of British Columbia opened a major student housing complex adjacent to what was then Totem Park, and named it after the park. Later, to commemorate its tenth anniversary, the Residents Association decided to replace the decaying house board that stood in front of the main entrance. Coast Salish carver Simon Charlie was commissioned to replicate it, and in 1974 it was installed with ceremony. Chief Tsem-lano of Musqueam and others from the band attended in ceremonial regalia.

A plaque at the base of the carved house board incorrectly refers to it as a welcome pole. The sculpture depicts a man facing a bear coming out of a cave. An interpretation of it was given to anthropologist Homer Barnett in 1936 by Chief Jack of Musqueam. It concerns a supernatural power that the chief said belonged to his grandfather. This man, a hunter, was able to mesmerize bears and other animals by singing a special song and shaking a rattle, enabling him to make a kill with ease. The carving shows a knife in the man's left hand and a rattle in his right.

The original house board, now in the university's Museum of Anthropology, does not have the adzed texture that Simon Charlie gave to the replica. Many years previously, he had bought a set of tools from an elderly man and used one of them to finish a sculpture with the technique he calls "feathering." "It changed my style," he said, "I don't like a smooth finish any more."

6 ft.
1.8 m

55

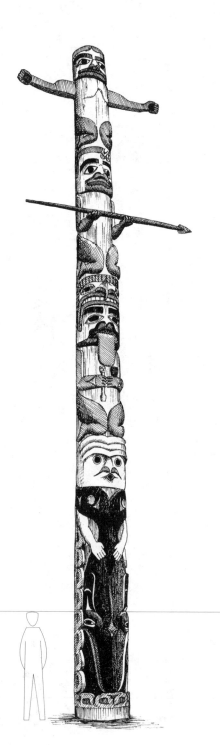

4 LOCATION: *Vancouver—Psychology Building, 2136 West Mall, University of British Columbia*
CARVER: *Art Thompson with Joe David*
CULTURAL STYLE: *Nuu-chah-nulth*

Although it is certainly not a house frontal pole, this tall carving nevertheless clings to the north face of a building on the University of British Columbia campus.

The carver cut the log on the Nitinat Reserve and worked on it at the village of Iithloo, his home, at the northwest end of Nitinat Lake on Vancouver Island. The pole was to fulfil a commission by the university's Museum of Anthropology for a Nuu-chah-nulth pole. The innovative work depicts aspects of the whale hunt, an ancient tradition unique to these people (and to their relatives, the Makah, of Washington State's Olympic Peninsula). "I carved the pole for all the Nuu-chah-nulth people," Thompson said, "and for their ancient whaling tradition."

The top figure depicts the harpooner (also called the whaler), a high-ranking chief who holds in his hands the tips of the dorsal fins from two whales. When brought to shore, the sea mammal was divided up among the whaling crew, and the chief received the dorsal fin; thus, this harpooner has taken two whales.

Beneath him is the man who holds second position in the seven-man crew and who sits behind the whaler. He ties inflated sealskin floats onto the harpoon line that holds the whale and pays out the line as the creature dives. He also retrieves the harpoon, which he is shown holding.

The next figure is that of the shaman, holding a baleen rattle in his left hand and a magical wand in his right. Shaking the rattle and singing a special song, or touching a harpooned whale with the wand, could cause it to turn in the right direction—towards the village, not out to sea. The shaman wears a hawk frontlet (or headdress) to indicate high rank, while the Lightning Snake emanating from his mouth symbolizes his strong inner powers. Notice the use of copper on the shaman's mouth and frontlet.

Puk-ubs is depicted beneath the shaman. He is the reincarnation of a drowned whaling crew member who was washed ashore, a man who had reached complete purification. Puk-ubs is represented by white, wrinkled skin and pursed lips, as he calls: "Buk Buk."

At the base of the pole is mighty Whale itself, head down, with a wave design signifying the shore. The pattern on the tail flukes represents the slashes cut in it to slow down the sea mammal's retreat out to sea. Similarly, red paint inside the pectoral fin shows that it too has been cut, forcing the whale to turn in the desired direction. Red in the blowhole indicates the target of the spears, which follow the harpoon for the final kill. "Sewing" the whale's jaw closed, to prevent water from entering the carcass and thus sinking it, is represented by the long thin line along its mouth.

The carver, Art Thompson, said that he felt he could not bring himself to create a ceremony for a pole-raising outside of his tribal territory, so the carving went, instead, to enhance the newly finished Psychology Building. After two years in storage, the pole was installed in 1984.

A traditional six-beam Haida plank house and a mortuary house with frontal poles, as well as a memorial and a mortuary pole, on the grounds of the Museum of Anthropology. PHOTOGRAPH BY BILL MCLENNAN, COURTESY MUSEUM OF ANTHROPOLOGY, UNIVERSITY OF BRITISH COLUMBIA

BACKGROUND TO THE MUSEUM OF ANTHROPOLOGY
UNIVERSITY OF BRITISH COLUMBIA
VANCOUVER

The fine collection of poles on the grounds of the University of British Columbia's Museum of Anthropology in Vancouver began in the late 1940s with some carved house posts collected from nearby Musqueam, the last of such poles left in the lower mainland of British Columbia. The plan called for a collection of carved poles to represent the province's main native cultural groups, in a natural setting amid plants important to native Indian peoples.

Good examples of poles from various areas of the coast were bought and shipped to Vancouver and Victoria for restoration. Kwakiutl totem pole carver Ellen Neel, who was living in Vancouver, was employed in 1949 to repair some of the damaged and decayed poles; but after working all summer on seven poles, she felt she had to return to her own work of carving for her retail store and on commission.

Ellen Neel's elderly uncle, Mungo Martin, a master carver from Alert Bay, had been visiting her in Vancouver. When asked if he would be interested in taking over the project, he readily agreed. But patching up rotted wood proved too time consuming, tedious and unsatisfying, so the decision was made to better employ his skills in carving replicas of the old poles and in creating new ones.

Several poles and a house frame formed the first unit of Totem Park, situated on a 1.2-ha (3-acre) wooded area beside Marine Drive, less than 1.6 km (1 mile) from their present site.

In 1959 Haida artist Bill Reid and Doug Cranmer, an experienced Kwakiutl carver, began an ambitious program of creating two houses and a group of Haida poles for the second unit of Totem Park. This major endeavour spanned two and a half years.

When the university's impressive new Museum of Anthropology opened in 1976, the plan called for a section of a Haida village to be situated at the edge of a pool, which would symbolize a beach front. For geological reasons, the pool was never built (white pebbles indicate its proposed area), but the plank houses and some of the totem poles were moved there from Totem Park. Additional poles, representing other coastal Indian cultures, have since been added to the attractive and appropriate setting of forest, sea and mountains.

5 LOCATION: *Vancouver—Museum of Anthropology, University of British Columbia*
CARVER: *Norman Tait*
CULTURAL STYLE: *Nishga (Tsimshian)*

6 ft.
1.8 m

In 1977 the Museum of Anthropology held a one-man exhibition of the work of Norman Tait, a Nishga carver from Kincolith (near Prince Rupert), whose father and grandfather were carvers. The exhibit included woodcarvings, silk-screen prints, and silver and gold jewellery. During its run, Norman demonstrated woodcarving by working on a small totem pole in the exhibition gallery, and it is this pole that stands beside the trail to the museum's outdoor display.

Backed by a setting of trees, the carving depicts the Tait family at that time. The carver himself is at the top holding Raven, a family crest. At the base, his wife Jessie is represented by her main crest, Frog. In between them are their two young children, Isaac and Valerie, holding hands. The girl has a traditional form of identification for a female: hair parted down the middle.

It is not unusual for this artist to include some cryptic detail in his work, and this pole carries a hidden message that will not be revealed for many years—"Long after I'm gone," Norman said. Beneath Raven's upper beak, which is attached separately, he carved an inscription that will become visible only when the pole ages and rots, and the beak falls away.

Meanwhile, young Isaac, who apprenticed under his father at an early age, has become a skilled carver in his own right and often assists Norman on major projects.

Eight years after the pole was raised, Jessie Tait died, and Norman now considers it a memorial to her, pausing to pay his respects whenever he passes that way.

59

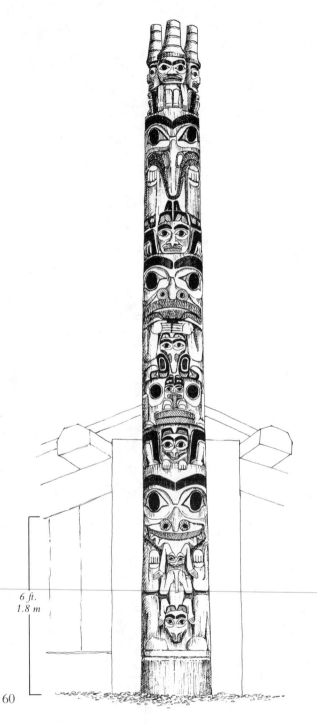

6 ft.
1.8 m

60

6 LOCATION: *Vancouver—Museum of Anthropology, University of British Columbia*
CARVER: *Bill Reid with Doug Cranmer*
CULTURAL STYLE: *Haida*

In 1957 Bill Reid was part of an expedition that went to Ninstints on remote Anthony Island, off the west coast of the Queen Charlotte Islands, to salvage totem poles that were endangered by continuing decay.

One particularly fine house frontal pole of 12.8 m (42 feet) had broken off at the ears of the bottom crest figure and was lying face-down in the moist earth. "We turned it over," Bill said, "expecting to find total decay, but to our delight the carving was intact except for some rot and a long crack." The fallen part, which was cut into two sections for transportation, together with the base figure, are on display inside the Museum of Anthropology.

Bill made a near copy of this pole, scaled down by a third, for the pole fronting the Haida mortuary house. "Since no trace of paint remained on the original," he said, "I followed tradition in painting certain areas of the carving in red and black." This complex and beautifully proportioned pole, finished in 1959, was the first of several that Bill would carve in the years ahead.

Three Watchmen are seated above Raven, who has arms and hands to signify his ability to transform into a human. A small face occupies Raven's upturned tail, while his claws emerge through the ears of Grizzly Bear, below. Filling the space on Grizzly Bear's chest is a small Raven, with a wing on each side of its beak. Beneath is Frog, wide eyed, with a small Mosquito between its eyes. Below Frog, a Bear cub crouches, its hind legs protruding through the ears of another Grizzly Bear, at the base of the pole. A Frog protrudes from Grizzly Bear's mouth, and there is a Wolf cub between his front and hind legs.

The structural remains of the large six-beam house that the original of this pole once fronted can still be seen at Ninstints.

7 LOCATION: *Vancouver—Museum of Anthropology, University of British Columbia*
CARVER: *Bill Reid with Doug Cranmer*
CULTURAL STYLE: *Haida*

The central focus of the museum's outdoor display is a large six-beam plank house, complete with house frontal pole—a replica of Haida dwellings of the late nineteenth century. When the sliding door at the side is open, visitors may go inside. On the back wall stands a massive house post with several carved and painted crests. A wide platform around the perimeter and a dirt floor are standard for such houses; smoke from fires rose through the open smoke hole in the roof. This house is used for special functions, during which salmon is often roasted in the nearby pit and served from the house.

Fronting the dwelling, which is made entirely of red cedar, is a tall, complex pole, its design inspired by a pole that once fronted a house at the south end of Skidegate on the Queen Charlotte Islands. The asymmetrical tail flukes of Dogfish rise above the three Watchmen, the central one of which holds onto the domed head of Dogfish, whose dorsal fin forms the Watchman's nose. In its characteristic downturned mouth, Dogfish holds a small Whale.

The next figure shows Frog protruding through the ears of Eagle, which is holding Sculpin to its chest, grasping in its claws the long spines that characterize sculpins.

At the base is Killer Whale, a blowhole on its forehead, and with a man crouched above the upturned tail flukes, a combination that tells of the Nanasimget story.

61

6 ft.
1.8 m

Impressed by the bold and powerful crest figures on poles collected from Skedans and Tanu on the Queen Charlotte Islands, Bill Reid carved a mortuary pole incorporating two of these figures to represent the Bear Mother story.

From the Tanu pole (sections of which are in the Museum of Anthropology), he recreated Grizzly Bear and its two cubs, and combined these with Bear Mother from a Skedans pole fragment. The upper figure is the Bear Mother, the lower is the Bear Chief; each parent holds a twin cub against its chest.

The frontal board at the top is Bill Reid's own creation and represents Eagle. In a classic split-design, the wings are placed at the top, with the leg and claws below, and the tail in the lower outer corners. However, with the knowledge now gained over many years of association with Haida culture, he points out that depicting Eagle was inappropriate, because this crest does not belong with th Bear Mother story.

As was customary with single mortuary poles, the broad end of the log is uppermost. This provided maximum width for the cavity behind the frontal board, to hold the box containing the remains of the deceased. Boards then covered the top of the cavity. As this mortuary pole was not intended to be functional, it has no cavity. The pole was on display at the Spokane World's Fair of 1974.

9 LOCATION: *Vancouver—Museum of Anthropology, University of British Columbia*
CARVER: *Jim Hart*
CULTURAL STYLE: *Haida*

Another example of classic Haida design is seen in the replica of a pole that once stood up against a house in Masset on the Queen Charlotte Islands, a village that bristled with some fifty poles during the late nineteenth century. Sometime before 1878 the house was abandoned, and in 1902 Dr. Charles F. Newcombe, a commercial collector of Indian art, bought the pole for the provincial museum in Victoria, B.C. It stood in Beacon Hill Park for many years until a windstorm sent it crashing, breaking the pole beyond repair. The pieces were given to the Museum of Anthropology and are now in storage.

The museum commissioned Jim Hart of Masset to replicate the pole, with Bill Reid acting as consultant. "I wanted to experience all aspects of carving the first pole for which I'd be responsible," Jim Hart said, "so I began by involving myself in choosing the cedar log." When some rot subsequently showed up, he adzed it out and carefully fitted in a section of good wood. For ten months he worked long and often lonely hours carving the pole.

At the top of the pole is Raven, Frog, Sea Bear with its cub, an upside-down human, Bear holding Frog in its mouth; small frogs peek through the ears of Grizzly Bear at the base, holding Sculpin.

Volunteers, after carrying Jim Hart's pole from the carving shed to the museum, lower it to the ground, 1982.
PHOTOGRAPH BY BILL MCLENNAN, COURTESY MUSEUM OF ANTHROPOLOGY, UNIVERSITY OF BRITISH COLUMBIA

10 LOCATION: *Vancouver—Museum of Anthropology, University of British Columbia*
CARVER: *Bill Reid with Doug Cranmer*
CULTURAL STYLE: *Haida*

A large double mortuary pole in an early photograph of Skidegate—once the home of Bill Reid's mother—provided the carver with inspiration and reference for this double mortuary pole.

The wide frontal board depicts the crest of Dogfish in a split-design that combines both two and three dimensions, one easily flowing into the other. The body of Dogfish carries the sharp spine and dorsal fin at the top, the pectoral fins on either side of the mouth, and the asymmetrical tail in each lower corner.

Originally, this double mortuary pole had the required boxlike structure for the remains of the deceased. In 1974 it was dismantled and shipped to the Spokane World's Fair for display. On its return, however, the planks forming the box were missing, so it was reassembled without this feature.

Doug Cranmer (left) *and Bill Reid use a variety of tools to carve the frontal boards of the double mortuary pole, around 1960.*
COURTESY MUSEUM OF AN-
THROPOLOGY, UNIVERSITY OF
BRITISH COLUMBIA

11 LOCATION: *Vancouver—Museum of Anthropology, University of British Columbia*
CARVER: *Bill Reid with Doug Cranmer*
CULTURAL STYLE: *Haida*

The last pole to complete the Haida village project was this memorial pole. There is a horizontal Raven atop the eight skils, and the base carries a monumental Beaver crest with a Bear cub between its ears. The cub, in a split-design, interlocks with Beaver by having a front and hind leg in each of the large ears.

Unable to obtain a log of sufficient girth and length for the massive pole he had in mind, Bill Reid carved Beaver as a separate piece, hollowing out the centre and back. It forms a sheath around the base of the pole.

Beaver is textured all over by adzing, the only figure on which Bill used this technique. The holes in the ringed section were created courtesy of pileated woodpeckers, from the nearby woods.

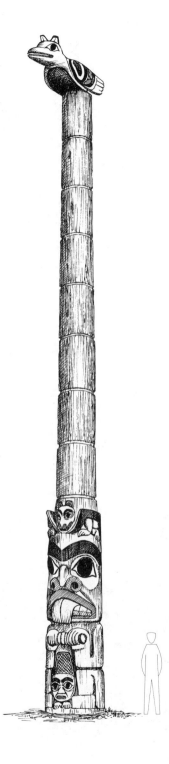

12 LOCATION: *Vancouver—Museum of Anthropology, University of British Columbia*
CARVER: *Mungo Martin*
CULTURAL STYLE: *Kwakiutl*

In addition to repairing some old poles for the Museum of Anthropology, master carver Mungo Martin created two new ones, completing both in 1951. They now stand on the grassy knoll directly behind the museum and are reflected in the glass walls of the Great Hall.

The pole on the west side was the subject of a short 16-mm film produced by the university. Entitled *Making a Totem Pole*, the film followed the process from raw log to finished pole and showed Mungo's mastery of using the adze in a wide variety of techniques.

This pole carries crests that Mungo, as a chief of Fort Rupert, was entitled to depict. At the top is the Cannibal Bird, or Hokw-hokw, followed by an Ancestral Chief holding Frog against him, followed by Bear holding a salmon; next, Killer Whale is depicted with its head downward. At the base is Beaver, chewing a stick, with the customary face on its tail joint.

Carver Mungo Martin uses the traditional "D" adze to sculpt a small face on this pole. COURTESY MUSEUM OF ANTHROPOLOGY, UNIVERSITY OF BRITISH COLUMBIA

13 LOCATION: *Vancouver—Museum of Anthropology, University of British Columbia*
CARVER: *Mungo Martin*
CULTURAL STYLE: *Kwakiutl*

The other pole by Mungo Martin completed in 1951 for the Museum of Anthropology was to commemorate Chief Kalilix, the head of Mungo's family line, who had obtained the privilege of being served first at potlatch feasts.

Although somewhere in his early sixties—his birth was not recorded—Mungo Martin worked diligently on the museum's totem pole project, without assistants. He would sing gently to himself or sometimes out loud, usually a song associated with the figure he was carving.

The crest figures on this pole show Thunderbird at the top, with its wings by its sides rather than outspread. Next is an Ancestral Chief, followed by Raven perched over Whale; notice the upside-down face in the inverted tail fluke, the protruding dorsal fin, and the head facing downward.

At the base stands another chief, possibly Chief Kalilix himself, with a blanket around his shoulders; the ceremonial head and neck rings he wears symbolize his rank.

Although much of the original paint has weathered away over the decades, it remains a fine pole, towering against a backdrop of coastal mountains.

14 LOCATION: *Vancouver—Museum of Anthropology, University of British Columbia*
CARVER: *Walter Harris and Richard Harris, with Doreen Jensen, Rodney Harris,*
   Vernon Stephens
CULTURAL STYLE: *'Ksan (Tsimshian)*

The pole at the north end of the museum's outdoor exhibit had its beginning with a series of half-hour made-for-TV films on traditional skills in various cultures. Sunrise Films of Toronto commissioned Walter Harris, a well-known 'Ksan carving instructor, to create a totem pole with his sixteen-year-old son, Richard. (Traditionally, a carver would train his nephew.) To meet the deadline, the carver's sister, Doreen Jensen, herself an accomplished carver, his older son, Rodney, and others also worked on the pole. The Royal Bank of Canada, which funded the work, donated the completed pole to the Museum of Anthropology.

For the pole raising on 24 August 1980, a large contingent of native people from the Hazelton and Kispiox area of northern British Columbia flew in to create a lavish ceremony, rich in the cultural traditions of the Gitksan. The pole was raised in three stages, marked by songs, speeches and dancing with masks. Hundreds of spectators helped to haul on the ropes, raising the pole to its upright position against a cloudless sky.

A pebble ceremony followed the Wolf dance. Those invited to the pole raising were asked to bring a pebble, which they threw into the excavated hole in which the pole was set. This gesture was symbolic of filling the hole with large rocks, as was done in early times, to buttress the base of the towering monument. All those attending then feasted on a salmon dinner served from the nearby Haida house.

The film crew flew in and documented the final phase of their project—the pole raising—but that night thieves broke into their truck and stole not only the equipment but the reels of film. With improvisation, the film was completed, but it lacked complete coverage of the colourful event.

The top of this unpainted pole carries the crest of Running Wolf, followed by Mosquito. Below is Killer Whale, with a dorsal fin and a blowhole on its forehead, and a pectoral fin on each side. Killer Whale is abducting a woman, crouched on its chest, whose pursuing husband is looking out from between the sea mammal's tail flukes: the Nanasimget story. At the base is Frog, with a small frog in its mouth.

The elaborately carved folding doors at the entrance to the Museum of Anthropology are also the work of 'Ksan carvers, who worked under the guidance of Walter Harris. The rich array of figures illustrates a legend that tells of the origin of the first Gitksan people on the Skeena River.

Participants in ceremonial attire watch the final stages of raising the 'Ksan pole at the Museum of Anthropology, 24 August 1980. PHOTOGRAPH BY HILARY STEWART

15 LOCATION: *Vancouver—Maritime Museum, north foot of Cypress St.*
CARVER: *Mungo Martin with Henry Hunt, David Martin*
CULTURAL STYLE: *Kwakiutl*

To mark the occasion of British Columbia's centenary in 1958, the province presented H.M. Queen Elizabeth with a superb totem pole towering nearly 30.5 m (100 feet) into the air, one foot for each year of the province's life. After the First Cut Ceremony, when Lt.-Gov. Frank M. Ross made the first cut into the log, it took native carvers almost seven months to complete the pole. It now stands majestically in Windsor Great Park, in England. The pole near the Maritime Museum is an exact duplicate of the one given to the queen.

The log for the original pole was an exceptionally fine 600-year-old red cedar from the Queen Charlotte Islands. The chief carver was Mungo Martin; his carving assistants were his son David Martin and his nephew Henry Hunt, who later became a renowned carver himself.

Each of the ten figures is the crest of one of the ten Kwakiutl clans, and each represents the mythical ancestor of that clan. Although it is difficult to see the top figures because of the height, the pole depicts the following: at the top, a chief wearing a high-crowned hat and robe, followed by Beaver, Old Man, Thunderbird and Sea Otter holding a seal. Next is Raven (tail uppermost), his downward head between the tail flukes of Whale—notice the face for the blowhole. Below, a woman is flanked by the body of Sisiutl, on whose central head she crouches. Next is Halibut (tail uppermost), having a human within its body; at the base is Cedar Man, wearing head and neck rings.

Backed by the panorama of rugged mountains, the glass-towered city and the ships plying the waters of English Bay, this cedar monument stands as a reminder of the province's early inhabitants.

The enormous cedar log for the centennial pole, brought to Victoria by train, being prepared for carving by Mungo Martin, Henry Hunt and Tony Hunt. COURTESY GOVERNMENT OF BRITISH COLUMBIA

6 ft./1.8 m

Although Don Yoemans had already established a reputation in his native art, this was only the second pole he had worked on. He has a strong sense of satire and very much a twentieth-century mind, and his work—even today—often incorporates whimsy and inventive imagery. His explanation of the pole he created for the college, perhaps an expression of student difficulties, goes thus:

"Top figure: The Bear represents the cruel world or the bogey man; between its ears, a little man with an open mouth symbolizes the people who tell you to stay on the beaten path and forget your crazy dreams.

"Centre figure: Here we have another Bear, without ears, devouring a man with a flute in his hand. This says, 'It doesn't matter how good you are, if no one hears, you are as good as dead.' I do not believe this applies to specific talent such as art or music; the only real talent people have is to express what is really inside themselves.

"Bottom figure: In early times a figure carved upside-down was a way of degrading a specific individual. Here we have a man being degraded and eaten by a large man. I call this figure 'man with ulcers,' because both figures are the same person. The large image secretly weeps as he eats himself up inside over dreams not pursued."

Don Yoemans has become a successful artist, carver and jeweller in Vancouver.

21 LOCATION: *Vancouver—Native Education Centre, 285 East 5th Ave.*
CARVER: *Norman Tait with Robert Tait, Isaac Tait, Wayne Young, Harry "Hammy" Martin*
CULTURAL STYLE: *Nishga (Tsimshian)*

This unpainted portal pole adds richness to the façade of the Native Education Centre.

The carved figures tell the story of Man, taken care of by the spirits, who wandered the empty earth. Lonely, he went to the forest and asked the Spirit of the Forest, "Why am I alone? Isn't there anyone in the forest to help me?" The spirit said, "I will give you Black Bear. If you can live in harmony with him, I will send you more of my children." He did, and Man learned to live in peace with the forest people.

Paddling on the sea, Man asked the Spirit of the Sea, "Why am I alone on the water?" The spirit said, "I will send you Blackfish; if you learn to live with him, I will send you more of my children." He did, and Man learned to live with the people of the sea.

Noticing the emptiness of the sky one day, Man said to the Spirit of the Sky, "Send me one of your children, for I have twice shown that I can live with other than myself." The Spirit of the Sky sent him Raven, and Man again proved he could live in harmony with the other creatures.

That humans can live together with the children of the forest, the water and the sky is evidenced by the many animals, fish and birds that still abound in these habitats. If we can learn to live in peace with such diverse creatures, we can surely live in peace with each other.

The Native Education Centre is a lively place for adult native Indian people who want to further their education. The innovative building, designed by architect Larry McFarlane and based on the traditional northern plank house, contains some of the largest hand-hewn planks and beams to be found in Canada. The landscaping includes plants traditionally used by native people for food, medicine and in technology. Each is labelled with its common English and scientific names, as well as its name in a Coast Salish dialect.

Norman Tait's carving assistants were all family: brother, son, nephew and cousin, and they are represented by the four faces around the entrance. Each man carved his own "signature piece"; though similar, all are different. Tait's signature piece is the delightful little bear cub. The pole is named Wilp, meaning "where the people gather." The building is also used for social events, with the entrance through the pole being used on special ceremonial occasions.

On 25 June 1985, the finished pole was raised in a ceremony rich with colourful regalia, speeches, dancing, drumming, singing, gift-giving and food for all, including deer meat stew. Photographer and writer Vickie Jensen made a complete documentation, in writing and photographs, of the pole and its carvers, from choosing the log to raising the finished pole.

Norman Tait's portal pole being raised at the Native Education Centre in Vancouver, 1985. PHOTOGRAPH BY HILARY STEWART

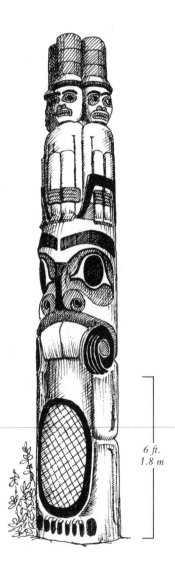

22 LOCATION: *Vancouver—House of Happiness, 860 East 7th Ave.*
CARVER: *Roy Hanuse*
CULTURAL STYLE: *Northern*

Standing as a sentinel in front of an attractive multiple-housing unit, this pole identifies one of many such units built by the Vancouver Native Housing Project, which provides quality accommodation for urban native Indian people. The rusty red and blue used on the building's exterior echo the colours on the pole, which stands in a landscaped garden, spotlit at night.

Each house has its own pole, carved by various native artists, and each features Beaver—the busy creature that builds its own home—topped by three Watchmen, or guardian spirits, who watch over the house. Each house also has a name, as did the large houses of old that sheltered many families under one roof. This one is named House of Happiness; another, for elders, is called House of Pearls.

6 ft.
1.8 m

23 LOCATION: *Vancouver—Plaza of Nations, 750 Pacific Blvd.*
CARVER: *Earl Muldoe with assistants*
CULTURAL STYLE: *'Ksan (Tsimshian)*

Clustered in an attractive setting, three totem poles look out over the Plaza of Nations—a legacy of the Expo 86 World's Fair in the heart of the city.

Originally these poles, together with two smaller ones, were commissioned by Highfield Development to grace the entrance to Airport Executive Park in Richmond, B.C. Seventeen years later they were taken down and donated to the Vancouver Museum. The two small poles went to the Vancouver Trade and Convention Centre, and the three tall ones to the Plaza of Nations—all on long-term loan.

Two of the poles in the plaza are by Earl Muldoe, a veteran carver of 'Ksan. "I personally selected the logs I wanted to use," he said. "These are old-growth cedars, with scarcely a knot on their entire length. They came from the Kitimat valley."

The Nanasimget story of the Whale abducting the man's wife is shown at the top of this pole: here the wife is riding Whale's tail. Beneath the crouched figure of the husband is Hawk, with its claws on a small human who fills the space between the ears of Owl, below.

Next is a legendary being who has his head on his chest, not on his neck; hence, the arms are shown coming from the sides of the man's head. This is a crest of the carver. The being holds Frog, and at the base is Eagle.

LOCATION: *Vancouver—Plaza of Nations, 750 Pacific Blvd.*
CARVER: *Walter Harris with assistants*
CULTURAL STYLE: *'Ksan (Tsimshian)*

One of the poles at the Plaza of Nations is by another veteran 'Ksan carver, Walter Harris. At the top of the pole, a human sits on the head of Eagle-Person, a crest said to have been taken by a family on its ancient migration from Hagwilget country to Kitwancool. In a lake they saw a large human being with an eaglelike head, wearing a headdress of grizzly bear claws that had water lily leaves around it: all these became crests.

The carving on the pole depicts this supernatural being with an eaglelike head, human arms holding a frog, wings carved with human heads, and legs that end in clawed feet. The outspread wings are an unusual feature for a 'Ksan pole.

Beneath is Grizzly Bear of the Sea; the two dorsal fins signify its marine affiliation. Variations in Sea Bear crests for this area also have three fins, or one fin with a carved face on it.

The Gitksan have a story similar to the Haida's Nanasimget story, in which Whale abducts a man's wife. The lower section of the pole portrays this: the wife is clinging to Whale's dorsal fin; its pectoral fins are at the sides, and the tail fluke is turned over its back. The husband is at the base.

25 LOCATION: *Vancouver—Plaza of Nations, 750 Pacific Blvd.*
CARVER: *Earl Muldoe with assistants*
CULTURAL STYLE: *'Ksan (Tsimshian)*

On the second pole by Earl Muldoe at the Plaza of Nations, a lone Watchman sits atop four rings, called "chief's rings" by the carver. "Each ring," he said, "had to be earned by the owner through some special undertaking or major commitment." Beneath the rings, Raven appears in his traditional duality—as bird and as human, with the latter crouched between the ears of Bear, who holds Frog before him. These are two separate crests carved in combination.

Bear's feet rest on the head of the supernatural Mountain Hawk. "He's always shown with both a recurved beak and a mouth with many teeth. It is a crest of my family," the carver said.

Also belonging to the Muldoe family is a very old crest known as Halfway Out, seen at the base of the pole. The origin of this goes back to the war expedition of the warrior Naeqt against the Kitimat people of the coast. In the early 1920s, his great-grandson gave an account of the gruesome event to Canadian anthropologist Marius Barbeau: "Naeqt started on the warpath against Kitimat. On his way down, he came upon a camp, wherein a man sat by himself. He took his knife and cut the man through the middle almost in two halves, so strong was he. The wounded man ran into the lake and stood in the water up to his ribs." The name and the crest Halfway Out were derived from this incident and brought back by the warrior.

81

6 ft.
1.8 m

26 LOCATION: *Vancouver—Canadian Broadcasting Corporation, 700 Hamilton St.*
CARVER: *Richard Hunt with Tim Paul*
CULTURAL STYLE: *Kwakiutl*

As work on this pole progressed, a lighthearted friendship sprang up between Richard Hunt, the chief carver, and Jane Wilson of the CBC's public relations department. Richard Hunt had originally intended to include on the pole a depiction of Bookwus, the Wild Man of the Woods. When he told Jane that he had decided instead to carve the female counterpart, Dzoonokwa, the Wild Woman of the Woods, and that it would represent her, she thought he was joking again.

Many CBC staff members attended the pole-raising ceremony in front of the CBC building, and as the carved cedar log slowly rose higher, Richard turned to Jane and said, "There you go!" Interestingly, this representation of Dzoonokwa (who is usually depicted without clothes) shows her wearing a skirt, perhaps as a courtesy to Jane.

The pole is topped by the mythical Kolus, a powerful giant bird and younger brother of Thunderbird. Beneath Kolus, Bear holds Dzoonokwa to his chest, and below them is the head of Sisiutl, the supernatural double-headed sea serpent.

BACKGROUND TO BROCKTON POINT IN STANLEY PARK
VANCOUVER

PHOTOGRAPH BY HILARY STEWART

In 1889, shortly before the great fire that all but wiped out the fledgling city of Vancouver, the Art, Historical and Scientific Association was born. An active organization, it put together the city's first museum, which included "Indian relics and handicrafts," and later decided to set up an Indian village in Stanley Park.

One suggestion for accomplishing this—reprehensible as it now seems—was that "some old deserted village should be purchased, transported to the site and re-erected." With that idea ruled out as impractical, the alternative was to buy the totem poles and build the houses.

Several poles were purchased and set up, but the village never materialized. To celebrate the city's golden jubilee in 1936, three more poles were added—a gift of the jubilee committee and the Department of Indian Affairs.

Over the years the totem pole collection in Stanley Park has changed considerably, with new ones added and deteriorating ones replaced or replicated.

Ignore the metal plaque with the obscure explanations of the various figures on the poles. But do take a look at the large boulder nearby, which is covered with petroglyphs—designs carved into the rock face (not pictographs as stated, which are paintings on rock).

In a dramatic grouping, backed by cedars and rugged mountains, floodlit at night, the crest figures and supernatural creatures of Stanley Park's totem poles contrast strongly with the modern glass-and-steel city that holds their gaze.

Two house posts, almost identical, are located in Stanley Park. Originally carved by Charlie James at the turn of the century, they were owned by Chief Tsa-wee-nok of Kingcome Inlet, their function being to support one of the crossbeams inside a large communal house. Another pair of house posts would have held a second beam, but it seems likely that the house was never built.

In 1914 the two posts were rented out to form part of a movie set built at Blunden Harbour for a full-length feature film about native Indian people on the Northwest Coast. Entitled *In the Land of the Head Hunters*, the movie was written and filmed by Edward S. Curtis, a photographer from Seattle, Washington, who spent a lifetime extensively documenting the Northwest Coast Indians, largely through his camera, recreating the old ways and appearances.

The Art, Historical and Scientific Association of Vancouver, continuing its program of acquiring totem poles for Stanley Park, bought the pair of house posts in 1927. Many years later, when one of them became badly decayed, it was replicated in Fibreglas and the original was stored at the Vancouver Museum. The Fibreglas pole is near the miniature railway in Stanley Park.

Many years of repainting had considerably changed the painted designs on the posts, so in 1988 when Tony Hunt carved a replica (left-hand pole) to replace the second post, he painted it with Charlie James's original designs, using an early photograph for reference. This pole is located at Brockton Point in Stanley Park.

Both house posts depict Thunderbird at the top, with Grizzly Bear holding a human at the base.

Film set of a Kwakiutl house interior, with the two carved house posts in position, for the shooting of Edward Curtis's 1914 film. PHOTOGRAPH BY EDMUND SCHWINKE, COURTESY UNIVERSITY OF WASHINGTON PRESS

29 LOCATION: *Vancouver—Stanley Park,*
CARVER: *Norman Tait with Robert Tait, Isaac Tait*
CULTURAL STYLE: *Nishga (Tsimshian)*

The legend of how the Tait family came to take Beaver for its crest is illustrated on this unusual pole and was told at its raising.

Long ago, five brothers (the five faces on the pole) of the Eagle people went hunting beaver for pelts, which were to be given away at a potlatch. Four of them went to the lake while the youngest stayed back to count the pelts. He noticed two beavers struggling upstream, gave them help, then followed them to their lodge in the lake. Peering down through the lodge's smoke hole (the cavity in the pole), he was amazed to see them take off their beaver skins and become men (the two figures beside the smoke hole).

"Our Beaver family is being slaughtered," they told their chief. "We must stop the killing." So the Beaver people all sang a sad song that caused the lake to freeze over; then they sang a happy song because they were now safe. Full of remorse for their actions, the Eagle people took Beaver for a crest and never again hunted these animals.

Other figures on the pole show, at the top, a man of the Eagle people (Tait's family) holding Raven, who shares the sky with him. The large figure beneath holds Frog in his right hand and Eagle in his left. They represent Norman Tait's son Isaac and his brother Robert, both experienced carvers who worked on the pole.

Part of the pole-raising ceremony included Isaac Tait performing the Squirrel dance along the top of the horizontal pole, and Norman Tait breathing life into the cedar log "to make it come alive," he said.

With speeches, singing and drumming, this large pole was raised by hand on 30 October 1987. Invited guests and casual park visitors hauled on the ropes to lift the carved log into place. The Tait family then provided food for everyone, as is customary.

30 LOCATION: *Vancouver—Stanley Park*
CARVER: *Ellen Neel*
CULTURAL STYLE: *Kwakiutl*

Traditionally, woodworking was, and with a few exceptions still is, the task of men. Ellen Neel was one of the exceptions. She came from a Kwakiutl family of carvers.

In 1955 Woodward's department store commissioned her to carve five totem poles for the new Westmount Mall in Edmonton, Alberta. With help from family members, the poles took shape beneath an awning-covered shed set up near her studio, called Totem Arts Studios, which she had opened in 1946 and where she sold her carvings in a thriving business. The studio was actually a World War II underground bunker in Stanley Park, one of many built to guard Vancouver against possible Japanese invasion. The area and minimal cement remains are marked by a plaque on a stone wall at Ferguson Point, near the Teahouse Restaurant.

Neel's poles stood in Edmonton for almost thirty years before three were returned to the coast, one as a gift to the University of British Columbia's Museum of Anthropology. The carver had died in 1966, but her son Robert renovated the pole, which is now on permanent loan to Stanley Park. The pole has truly come home.

The pole carries a selection of familiar Kwakiutl crests and is topped by Eagle. Beneath, Sea Bear has his feet on the shoulders of a woman (holding a frog), who stands on the head of Bookwus, the Wild Man of the Woods. Below, Dzoon-okwa crouches between the ears of Raven, whose beak is downturned on his chest.

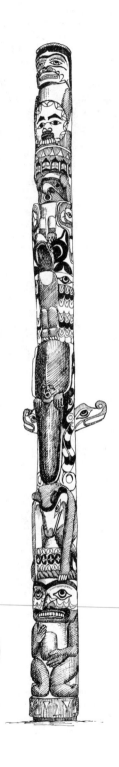

31 LOCATION: *Vancouver—Stanley Park*
CARVER: *Art Thompson and Tim Paul*
CULTURAL STYLE: *Nuu-chah-nulth*

For a long time, well-known carvers Art Thompson and Tim Paul had wanted to create a totem pole that would represent all the Nuu-chah-nulth people. Questioning the validity of a replica pole they had earlier been commissioned to make, Tim said, "We wanted to carve a pole that would speak of our people's legends and traditions, yet be our own contemporary statement." The result is this unusual pole, added to the Stanley Park group of totems in 1989.

At the top is Sky Chief, holding Moon; below Sky Chief's skirt is Kingfisher, its clawed feet touching the symmetrical tail flukes of Humpback Whale. Riding on Whale's back is Thunderbird—feathered wings at each side—being dragged underwater by Whale. Often a whale's blowhole is depicted as a face, and here it is imaginatively shown with a pair of hands also.

Flanking each side of Humpback Whale's long snout is Lightning Snake, a mythical creature with the head of a wolf, who assists Thunderbird in catching whales, on which it feeds. The Wolf below is carved in the style of Jimmy John, as a way of acknowledging this well-known Nuu-chah-nulth carver of the past.

The base depicts Man of Knowledge holding a wooden object, which Tim called a *tupati*, describing how it was used in certain marriage privileges such as games or tests of skill or courage. In this game, a man from the bridegroom's party threw the ball-like object into a crowd of men, who scrambled to retrieve it. The first person to run to the chief with it received a prize. At the same time, a smaller "ball" was thrown to a group of women who did likewise.

32 LOCATION: *Vancouver—Stanley Park*
CARVER: *Bill Reid with Werner True*
CULTURAL STYLE: *Haida*

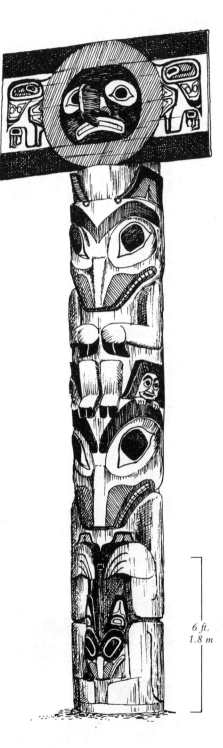

The only Haida pole among the carved columns in Stanley Park is this mortuary pole, which is a replica. The original pole was raised in Skidegate, Queen Charlotte Islands, sometime prior to 1878, to honour Chief Skedans, head chief of the abandoned village of Skedans, who had moved to Skidegate. Chief Skedans and his wife spent years accumulating the necessary money and gifts required for the lavish potlatch given at the pole raising. At the back of the pole were carved twenty-three short horizontal lines to record the number of blankets given away at the potlatch: each line represented twenty blankets, which cost two dollars each.

In 1936 the city of Vancouver celebrated its golden jubilee. As a gesture of recognition of its native people, the jubilee committee bought the pole from Henry Moody, the then Chief Skedans, for $100.

As the old pole deteriorated over the years, it was patched with plaster and cement, and was badly repainted in nontraditional colours. In 1964 the Vancouver Parks Board commissioned Bill Reid to carve a replica. Since there were few native carvers around at that time, Reid took on Werner True, a young German interested in Northwest Coast Indian art and a speedy woodworker, as his assistant. Between them they finished the pole in a month, with Reid receiving $1,500 and his assistant $1,000. Fragments of the original pole lying nearby in the bush have all but rotted away.

The frontal board at the top depicts Moon, with the face of Thunderbird, whose wings, legs and claws are painted on each side in a split-design. Beneath is Mountain Goat, identified by cloven hooves and two curved horns (now fallen off and not illustrated) on top of its head. At the base, Grizzly Bear holds what is probably Seal. All were crests of Chief Skedans.

6 ft.
1.8 m

89

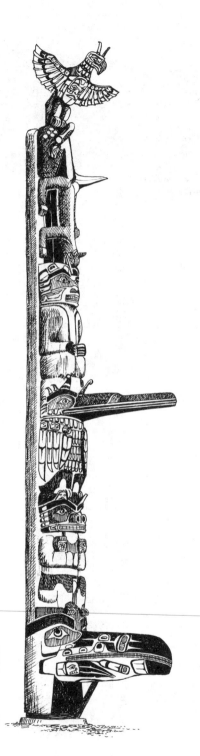

33 LOCATION: *Vancouver—Stanley Park*
CARVER: *Doug Cranmer*
CULTURAL STYLE: *Kwakiutl*

One of the first of the elaborate poles to be raised in Alert Bay was a memorial to Chief Wakius (or Wakas), which also served as a house frontal pole. Entry was through Raven's open mouth at the base of the pole. The memorial's design, which represents the Wakius family history in a long and complex legend, was developed from the speaker's staff (or talking stick) belonging to the chief. The pole was created by a carver named Yuxwayu, who received 350 blankets (valued at $515) in payment for his work.

The pole was raised prior to the mid–1890s, and a few years later an enormous beak was added to the open mouth of Raven. The upper beak was actually the prow of a canoe, upside-down; the lower beak was carved to fit. Projecting an estimated 2.7 m (9 feet), the beak opened to create an impressive ceremonial entrance into the house, the lower half dropping to form a ramp. The beak is shown here in its normal closed position. A door for daily use was installed to the left of the pole. By September 1900, outspread wings, a tail and legs had been painted on the house front to complete the monumental Raven. The well-known British Columbia artist Emily Carr made a painting of this pole in 1903 when she visited Alert Bay.

In 1928 the Art, Historical and Scientific Association of Vancouver bought the pole for $700—raised by public subscription—and shipped it to Stanley Park. Some sixty years later, the deteriorating pole was taken down and sent to Ottawa for conservation. Over the years the old pole had been repainted several times, drastically altering the original design. Through the use of early photographs, the pole was restored as nearly as possible to its original appearance. It became part of the Canadian Museum of Civilization's Northwest Coast exhibit, where it again fronts a Kwakiutl plank house.

In return, Stanley Park received a replica of the Wakius pole, carved by Doug Cranmer, who also supervised the restoration of the old pole. On 31 May 1987 a large gathering assembled at the base of the new Wakius pole, bright with fresh paint, for the dedication ceremony. Among the special guests resplendent in their crested button blankets were many native people from Alert Bay, including a number of descendants and relatives of Chief Wakius. Speeches, dancing, singing and drumming were followed by a feast for everyone who had witnessed the event.

A dramatic Thunderbird holding Whale in its claws crowns the top of the pole; below is Wolf (head down), one of the ancestors of Chief Wakius. Beneath is Wise One, a man of myth, followed by Hokw-hokw; below is Bear—notice the carved faces on its paws.

The original Wakius memorial pole in Alert Bay in the 1920s, with Raven's wings, tail and legs painted on the house front; notice the upside-down canoe prow used for Raven's upper beak. COURTESY VANCOUVER PUBLIC LIBRARY, NO. 4196

91

6 ft.
1.8 m

34 LOCATION: *North Vancouver—Carson Graham Secondary School, 2145 Jones St.*
CARVER: *Warren Smith with William Watts, Edward Baker*
CULTURAL STYLE: *Northern*

As there are two reserves and a large native Indian population in North Vancouver, Carson Graham School generally has about a hundred native students. In 1983 the vice-principal, Larry Brown, and the native student counsellor, Wally Sosnowski, came up with the idea of having students create a totem pole for the school.

A large cedar log was donated and, with great difficulty, was manoeuvred into the school's central courtyard. Research for the project included inviting Bill Reid to talk about native design and to inspect the log. Students in the Native Studies course submitted design sketches, and the one chosen was by Warren Smith (a non-native) and William Watts, a Squamish native, as was Edward Baker who joined the team of carvers. All had had some background in small woodcarving.

The boys worked mostly in their spare time on weekends and evenings, with occasional help from other students and plenty of help for the final painting. After eighteen months' work, on 17 April 1985, the twentieth anniversary of the school, the erected pole was unveiled at a ceremony that involved several elders of the Squamish Band.

The pole is topped by Eagle (wings folded), the crest of the school, with Whale beneath and Bear at the base, and was painted red and black. In 1990, white paint was added to negative areas to "brighten it up."

Master carver Bill Reid, with students of Carson Graham School, checks out the cedar log they will carve and talks about design.
COURTESY CARSON
GRAHAM SCHOOL

BACKGROUND TO THE "ROUTE OF THE TOTEMS" SERIES OF POLES
BRITISH COLUMBIA

In 1966 British Columbia celebrated the centennial of the joining of the colonies on Vancouver Island with the mainland settlements to form the province of British Columbia.

One of the more imaginative ideas of the centennial committee was to involve the province's native Indian people in a large-scale carving project.

Entitled "Route of the Totems" (also, for a while, "Route of the Haidas"), the project involved eleven carvers (with assistants), who were commissioned to create nineteen totem poles to be placed along tourist routes from Victoria to Prince Rupert. The poles were to be about 3.5 m (12 feet) in height, and 1 m (3½ feet) in diameter at the base. To bring unity to the variety of carving styles, the dominant figure on each pole was to be an upright Bear, with a secondary figure appropriate for the area for which it was carved.

To encourage high quality work, the provincial government held a contest, and anthropologist Wilson Duff of the provincial museum helped to judge the three best poles in the series.

Each pole at its installation was officially unveiled at a dedication ceremony with the carver present. The poles stand in villages and towns, along highways and at ferry terminals—most of them on Vancouver Island.

A selection of the "Route of the Totems" poles follows, according to their geographic location.

NOTE: The Kwakiutl Arts and Crafts Organization is credited with carving several of these poles. This group was established in 1965 by James Sewid of Alert Bay to encourage Kwakiutl artists and carvers to develop and maintain their artistic traditions, as well as to provide a commercial outlet for their work.

6 ft.
1.8 m

35 LOCATION: *West Vancouver—Centennial Park in Horseshoe Bay, "Route of the Totems"*
CARVER: *Tony Hunt*
CULTURAL STYLE: *Haida*

Situated between sheer mountains on one side and the small town of Horseshoe Bay on the other is a major B.C. Ferry terminal, with a "Route of the Totems" pole in Centennial Park on the waterfront nearby.

As a young carver in the early 1950s, Tony Hunt had worked with Kwakiutl carver Mungo Martin in the replication of a Haida pole in Victoria—there being no Haida carvers in those early years. The young carver, himself a Kwakiutl, said, "I chose to design the Horseshoe Bay pole in the Haida style, in part to confirm my ability to work in the northern style." Drawing from the heritage of his great-great-grandfather, a Tlingit, he incorporated the bold Grizzly Bear, and carved a Bear cub crouched between its ears, with the cub's legs protruding through Grizzly's ears. At the base, he added a high-ranking person wearing a ringed hat.

Also in Horseshoe Bay, on the marina side of the bay, is the Boathouse Restaurant, with two beautiful panels, carved by Norman Tait in 1981, beside the main doors. The figures represent the four main crests of his people, the Nishga: these are Raven, Wolf, Eagle, and Killer Whale.

36 LOCATION: *Sechelt—community hall, Sechelt Indian Reserve*
CARVER: *Jamie Jeffries with Dwayne Martin, Howard Paul, Martin Baptiste*
CULTURAL STYLE: *Personal with Kwakiutl overtones*

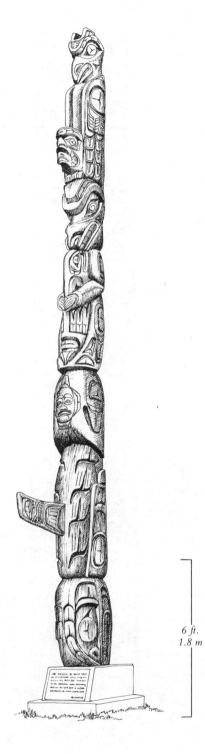

6 ft.
1.8 m

The Sechelt Band (Coast Salish) has an interesting assemblage of totem poles fronting its modern community hall. Although the Coast Salish were not traditionally totem pole carvers, the Sechelt people used this medium to express and document twenty years of frustration and struggle in trying to gain self-government.

A circle of seven carved standing figures represents three native people facing four faceless people who are government bureaucrats. One of the native people, a chief, carries a fully carved talking stick. In the centre of the circle, a large boulder displays a plaque telling how, in traditional times, the talking stick signified the authority of the one holding the stick to lead the people. The inscription continues: "Today our lives are dictated by the policies of the INDIAN ACT and enforced by the DEPARTMENT OF INDIAN AFFAIRS . . . OTTAWA. We continue to struggle for our forefathers . . . and for a better future."

Eventually the Sechelt Band became the first band in Canada to obtain self-government, and the Band Council makes its own decisions and policies. The people now carry their own talking stick.

To celebrate and document this important milestone, two poles were carved—one in recognition of the federal government's decision, the other in recognition of the provincial government's co-operation. Illustrated here is the latter pole, which was unveiled on 24 June 1988. As the premier of British Columbia read out the words on the plaque at the base of the pole, Chief Thomas Paul repeated them for all to hear: "In celebration of practicality, good will and reasonableness, showing what can be achieved when governments work together. This pole was unveiled during the inauguration ceremony for the Sechelt Indian Government District, a new form of government in Canada."

Eagle looks down from the top of this pole and has a Wild Man of the Woods mask at his feet; below is Bear, clasping a salmon. The lower half of the pole depicts Whale, head down, with a Sun design on its turned-back tail flukes and a carved face on its dorsal fin.

95

6 ft.
1.8 m

37 LOCATION: *Tsawwassen—causeway to Tsawwassen Ferry Terminal, "Route of the Totems"*
CARVER: *Sam Henderson*
CULTURAL STYLE: *Kwakiutl*

This pole of the "Route of the Totems" group marks the entry to the Tsawwassen Ferry Terminal causeway. Ferries leave from the terminal for Swartz Bay and Nanaimo on Vancouver Island and for the Gulf Islands.

The pole, which stands to the left of the road, looks out across the sea. At the top of the pole is the required Grizzly Bear (holding a fish), with Eagle at the base. It is one of the many poles carved by Sam Henderson of Campbell River.

38 LOCATION: *Swartz Bay—Swartz Bay Ferry Terminal, "Route of the Totems"*
CARVER: *Henry Hunt*
CULTURAL STYLE: *Kwakiutl*

The ferry from Tsawwassen on the mainland to Victoria on Vancouver Island arrives at the Swartz Bay Ferry Terminal, which also serves the Gulf Islands. In front of the terminal's coffee shop is a fine, unpainted carving of Grizzly Bear and Whale.

This is one of three poles in the "Route of the Totems" series created by Mungo Martin's son-in-law, Henry Hunt. At Mungo's death in 1962, Henry was appointed chief carver at the British Columbia Provincial Museum in Victoria, where he remained for fourteen years. His skill in carving monumental and ceremonial pieces was, at the time, without equal, and his output prodigious.

First prize in the "Route of the Totems" contest was awarded to this pole. The carver's son, Tony Hunt, believed this was the finest piece his father carved; he called it "state of the art Kwakiutl carving."

On this powerful pole is Grizzly Bear, with Whale's head resting on Bear's chest, pectoral fins at each side; Whale's blowhole is represented as an upside-down head, while the dorsal fin appears immediately below, flat against its body. Notice how the design carved into the sea mammal's tail flukes forms a face, also upside-down.

6 ft.
1.8 m

97

39 LOCATION: *Sidney—Washington State Ferries Terminal, Ocean Ave., "Route of the Totems"*
CARVER: *Tony Hunt*
CULTURAL STYLE: *Kwakiutl*

Passengers arriving in Sidney on Vancouver Island off the ferry from Washington are greeted by another of the "Route of the Totems" poles, this one atop a sloping flower bed bearing the words: WELCOME TO SIDNEY, B.C.

Prior to starting this commission, Tony Hunt had been at the British Columbia Provincial Museum, working on a replica Gitksan pole that had a large frog on it. For the Sidney pole, he felt he wanted to do "one powerful Bear," and influenced by his recent work, decided to add a large Frog for the required second figure.

Because it was still early in his carving career, he made a model of the pole before tackling the 3.7-m (12-foot) log. Afterwards, he gave the model to Laurie Wallace, then deputy provincial secretary, who was responsible for the "Route of the Totems" program. This led to a request by Wallace for the carver to make more model totem poles, which were given to visiting dignitaries of note. "I used to call them my VIP poles," Tony said.

This pole is painted in brown, white, blue/green, red and black, leaving no wood unpainted, as is often the case with Kwakiutl totem poles.

6 ft.
1.8 m

40 LOCATION: *Victoria—Inner Harbour, Government St. and Belleville St., "Route of the Totems"*

CARVER: *Henry Hunt*

CULTURAL STYLE: *Kwakiutl*

6 ft.
1.8 m

Another pole in the "Route of the Totems" series stands in the heart of Victoria, British Columbia's capital city, on Vancouver Island.

This much-photographed pole is the powerful Bear, capped by Frog between its ears, holding a copper in its mouth and paws. At the base is a Hamatsa dancer wearing the ceremonial red cedar bark head and neck rings.

Henry Hunt, the best and the fastest of the carvers at the time, was commissioned to create three poles in the series. The other two, at Port Hardy and Swartz Bay, are also in this book. These carvings perpetuate the memory of a great chief and a fine artist and carver, whose three sons have continued in their father's tradition, becoming distinguished artists and carvers in their own right. Indeed, the Hunt family tree includes twenty-two men and women from three generations who practise traditional artistic skills in one form or another.

41 LOCATION: *Victoria—Royal British Columbia Museum, main entrance*
CARVER: *Henry Hunt and Tony Hunt*
CULTURAL STYLE: *Haida*

Dr. Charles F. Newcombe photographed it in 1901, Emily Carr painted it in 1928, the British Columbia Provincial Museum collected it in 1954, and Henry Hunt and Tony Hunt carved a replica of it in 1966.

This house frontal pole, one of the great masterworks from Tanu, the Haida village in the Queen Charlotte Islands renowned for the design and quality of its poles, once stood before a large plank house named House That Makes a Noise, owned by Gwiskunas.

The pole carries three Watchmen at the top, two of them with their legs and hands protruding through the ears of Eagle, below, a crest of the house owner's wife. Between Eagle's wings is the head of Hawk (or possibly Horned Owl), and between Eagle's curled talons is a Hair Seal.

Several different interpretations and names have been recorded for the next figure, which is a crest: Weeping Woman, Volcano Woman, Sea Anemone and Salt Water or Sea Chief. There is a good indication that the latter name is the correct one for this figure. The story associated with it (recorded by Newcombe during his visit to the Queen Charlotte Islands) is about Sea Chief, who lived close to a small island near the north end of Bank's Island, across the strait from Tanu. Each night his eyes fell out and hung suspended from a ligature; his lids closed over the sockets. So that he could see to eat, his friends put his eyes back in place, held them there, and propped his lids open. The Sea Chief's food consisted mainly of hair seals, but not having any teeth, he swallowed them whole, later spitting out the bones and other undigested parts, expelling them with great force. The eyeballs are depicted as small, crouching humans.

On the Sea Chief's chest is Frog, facing downward. Beneath is a human grasping the tail of Killer Whale, whose dorsal fin is between the knees of another human, shown upside-down, riding on Killer Whale's back. This trio tells of the Nanasimget story.

The downward head of Killer Whale becomes the head of Sea Bear, at the base of the pole. He is swallowing a sea mammal head first, with the flippers protruding from the sides of his mouth. Small animals peek through Sea Bear's ears as a filler.

The original house frontal pole (second from left) *stands against a large six-beam house, still intact in 1901.*
PHOTOGRAPH BY CHARLES NEWCOMBE, COURTESY ROYAL BRITISH COLUMBIA MUSEUM, PN 104

6 ft.
1.8 m

42 LOCATION: *Victoria—Royal British Columbia Museum, courtyard*
CARVER: *Richard Hunt*
CULTURAL STYLE: *Kwakiutl*

The courtyard in front of the Royal British Columbia Museum has a fine example of the Kwakiutl carver's art. The pole is by Richard Hunt, son of the renowned carver Tony Hunt, grandson of famed carver Henry Hunt and nephew of Mungo Martin. The museum commissioned the pole, the first the young carver did without consulting with his father. "When I came to a problem, I figured it out for myself," he said.

As with all the poles he carves, he uses only crests and prerogatives that belong to the Hunt family—and there are many. At the top, in spite of the eaglelike ears, stands Kolus, whose great claws are clasping the head of a chief wearing a Sun mask. This represents a family prerogative: during the Peace Dance, a chief leaves the dance house and later returns, transformed, as Sun. The Sun mask has Hawk Man's beak and long decorative rays emanating from the face. The chief, holding a copper in his hands and wearing a cedar bark dance skirt, stands on the head of Bear, between its ears.

The man being held in front of Bear is George Taylor (nicknamed "Slash"), a long-time friend of the carver. When he was a boy in Alert Bay, "Slash" and another boy played a reckless game with a sharp axe. Taking turns, each laid a finger on a chopping block while the other brought down the axe as close to it as he dared. Predictably, the blade veered off course and George lost half the index finger of his left hand. "Slash" grew up to become a famous soccer player for the Victoria Thunderbirds, an all-native Indian team that played across British Columbia. Hunt's likeness of his good friend is complete with moustache and chopped finger.

The carver knew that his work, raised in 1979, was a success when his elderly uncle, Tommy Hunt, sitting on a nearby bench, said to him: "I really like that pole. I like looking at it. I could sit here all day looking at it."

BACKGROUND TO THUNDERBIRD PARK
VICTORIA

A portion of Thunderbird Park, Victoria, showing Mungo Martin's house with its painted front, and two totem poles, 1986. COURTESY BRITISH COLUMBIA ARCHIVES AND RECORDS SERVICE, PN 16827

On the southwest corner of Douglas and Belleville Streets in Victoria, city lots C, D and E were vacant. The year was 1940, and the director of the nearby British Columbia Provincial Museum (now the Royal British Columbia Museum) had the novel idea of setting up a display of totem poles and canoes from the museum's collection on the empty corner. The public liked what they saw, and a letter to the director said, "Your totem pole exhibit a very good idea, and in an appropriate spot." Thus did the seed of Thunderbird Park begin to germinate.

Twelve years later it became obvious that continued exposure to wind and weather was causing deterioration to the poles, and they were taken indoors. The museum's curator of anthropology, Wilson Duff, was instrumental in setting up a major totem pole restoration program, often persuading business companies to donate cedar logs, lumber, trucking, shipping and more.

Mungo Martin, who for two years previously had been carving for the University of British Columbia's restoration program, began replicating many of the decaying old poles brought down from upcoast. A large carving shed was built so that the public could watch the new poles taking shape under the master carver's adze. This innovative idea fascinated visitors, who made such comments in a guest book as: "I could watch this Indian carve all day," and "This is damn nice but hell I forgot my camera!"

Mungo Martin also built a traditional Kwakiutl house, complete with Thunderbird crest house posts inside. On 16 December 1954 the house was opened with great ceremony, including the performance of more than seven dances, all belonging to Martin's family lineage.

Thunderbird Park continues to change as deteriorating poles are removed and new ones, created on site by skilled contemporary carvers, are added to city lots C, D and E, which are now well landscaped.

6 ft.
1.8 m

43 LOCATION: *Victoria—Thunderbird Park*
CARVER: *Mungo Martin*
CULTURAL STYLE: *Kwakiutl*

This carving is a replica of a house post, raised around 1870, which supported the central beam of a house at Koskimo, Quatsino Sound, on the northwest coast of Vancouver Island. The original post was collected in 1913 and for many years stood in the grounds of Government House in Victoria, the official residence of the lieutenant-governor of British Columbia.

At the top of the post is the head of Hokw-hokw, a crest obtained by the owner through his marriage to a woman of Kingcome Inlet. Originally, the mythic bird had outspread wings, as did the replica, and remnants of these are visible at either side of the post. Below Hokw-hokw is a humanlike being named Komokwa, or Copper Maker. As ruler or guardian of the Undersea, he lived in a marvellous house beneath the water and had live sea lions for house posts guarding the entrance. The dwelling housed much wealth, with many boxes filled with food, blankets, coppers and other treasures. Those seeking wealth who approached the house might be escorted in by a Whale. After a lengthy stay that seemed to be only a few hours, the visitor returned home in a canoe loaded with wealth goods.

On this house post, Komokwa is seen with a copper in his mouth—eating or breaking it—and his right hand in the mouth of a small Whale, profiled to the right, beneath him.

44 LOCATION: *Victoria—Thunderbird Park*
CARVER: *Mungo Martin with assistants*
CULTURAL STYLE: *Haida*

The village of Tanu on the Queen Charlotte Islands was once renowned for its superbly designed and carved house frontal, memorial and mortuary poles. One of these, collected in 1911, has been replicated in precise detail and stands outdoors with the clean lines and freshness of paint that the original once had.

The exact interpretation of this house frontal pole has been lost, but the familiar figures can still be recognized. Three Watchmen at the top stand guard over the house—two with their lower limbs protruding through the ears of Eagle below them. An upside-down head fits neatly between the ears of a humanlike figure who may well be Dzelaqons holding a Frog.

Dzelaqons, a niece of legendary Salmon-Eater, married a prince of the Grizzly Bear people and had children. The oral history telling of her place in Haida lore is long and involved, giving rise to other names for her: Frog Woman, Mountain Woman, Copper Woman and Volcano Woman.

The large creature at the base is Whale, with pectoral fins at each side; its hind end, with dorsal fin and tail flukes, is turned up onto its body. Whale's blowhole is defined by the head of an upside-down human figure. This figure may pertain to the Nanasimget story, or may, following tradition, be a means of ridiculing a person or family who owed a debt to the owner of the pole.

6 ft.
1.8 m

105

LOCATION: *Victoria—Thunderbird Park*
CARVER: *Mungo Martin with assistants*
CULTURAL STYLE: *Kwakiutl*

The heraldic pole customarily displayed the crests of the owner of the house, but this pole, carved by Mungo Martin, carries the crests of four of the tribes, or groups, that form the Kwakiutl nation.

Perched on top is Thunderbird, the crest of a clan (a group of related families) at Knight Inlet whose original ancestor was the Thunderbird who transformed into a man. Below is Grizzly Bear (holding a copper), who was the ancestor of a Kwakiutl clan, and below him is Grizzly Bear in human form. Next is Beaver, ancestor of a group at Blunden Harbour, and at the base is the giantess Dzoonokwa, a crest of a clan of the Nimpkish people. According to clan tradition, a man who chased Dzoonokwa for stealing dried fish eventually married her, and their son, half man and half Dzoonokwa, was the founder of the clan. He is seen at the base of the pole being held by his mother and looking back over his shoulder.

The house behind the pole is an authentic though scaled-down replica of a Kwakiutl house built at Fort Rupert in about 1853 by Chief Naka'penkim, Mungo Martin's uncle. Mungo was born in the old house and later inherited his uncle's position and assumed his name; thus, he took special pride in building the replica. Inside are four house posts, two at the back and two at the front, carved with the crests of three clans to which Naka'penkim was related by heredity or marriage. The painting on the house front represents a supernatural sea monster in the form of Bullhead (or Sculpin), and is taken from the house front design of a chief who was distantly related to Mungo.

The house in Thunderbird Park was opened in mid-December 1953 with three days of ceremony, to which the general public was invited on the third day. Notice of the occasion stated that it "will mark the first time this ancient Indian ceremony has been staged in the open in British Columbia since the Canadian government banned the practice in 1880." (It was actually banned in 1884.)

The elaborate affair was attended by native people from all over the coast. It brought back many of the ancient and complex ceremonies of the Kwakiutl potlatch, one of which saw Mungo Martin, as the owner of the house, give gifts to some thirty high-ranking people and tokens to around two hundred guests of lesser standing.

Masked dancers, representing Raccoon and Mouse (part of the Animal Kingdom presentation) dance around the central fire in Mungo Martin's plank house during the opening celebrations in 1953. COURTESY ROYAL BRITISH COLUMBIA MUSEUM, NO. 7038

When fire gutted the Thunderbird Park carving shed in 1980, it took with it a nearby Haida totem pole carved fifty-five years earlier. The shed was rebuilt in the style of a six-beam Haida house, with a frontal pole that is a replica of an old pole with quite a history.

The original was carved for a house named Rock Slide House, built sometime after 1878 in the village of Cumshewa on Moresby Island in the Queen Charlotte Islands. In 1901, with the village abandoned, collector Dr. Charles F. Newcombe of Victoria purchased the pole from the owners and sent it to the Field Museum of Natural History in Chicago. During the 1930s the Field Museum sold the pole to the Salvation Army, which erected it at a children's camp in Illinois. A collector from the eastern United States realized its value and bought it from the Salvation Army in the 1960s. In 1982 the National Museum of Man (now the Canadian Museum of Civilization) purchased the pole and brought it back to Canada.

On 9 June 1984 the magnificent new pole, replicated in the carving shed over eight months, was raised with ceremony. The invited public hoisted the 12.2-m (40-foot) column by hauling on ropes in traditional fashion, and the event was validated by speeches from representatives of the Haida nation with a performance by Haida dancers. Key among those invited, and splendidly attired in ceremonial blanket and headdress, was Charlie Wesley, the hereditary chief of Cumshewa.

At the top of the pole sit three Watchmen; below is Cormorant, looking somewhat human with arms and fingers, but with feathers at his elbows. Beneath Cormorant, in a complex interlocking design, is Whale, with a woman clinging to his tail flukes that lie on either side of her face. Whale's dorsal fin protrudes above its blowhole, which is represented by the head of a small upside-down human. These figures likely tell the story of Nanasimget. At the base stands Grizzly Bear, holding what are probably his twin cubs from the Bear Mother story.

47 LOCATION: *Victoria—Thunderbird Park*
CARVER: *Not known*
CULTURAL STYLE: *Gitksan (Tsimshian)*

According to an elder of long ago, a chief named Tu'pesu, who raised the original of this pole, could not afford the large expense such an event involved, so he entered into partnership with his longstanding friend Wawralaw, also a chief. Thus, the pole was jointly erected by them in 1855 at Kitsegukla on the Skeena River.

The name of the cedar monument is Great Being from the Lake, and it is this figure, wearing the Brave's Helmet, who tops the pole. Running through the headgear is a stick on which two Real Kingfishers are perched. All of these are family crests or emblems.

Below the uncarved length of pole is Hanging Frog, a crest probably derived from a legend about Neegyamks, a chief's daughter who disappeared one night. She was missing for two years, until one day two Frogs from the nearby lake appeared in the chief's doorway and led the people to the lake. With the help of neighbours, the lake was drained, whereupon a huge number of small Frogs took flight. The legend continues at length, telling of the death of Neegyamks and of her father killing a large Frog and taking it for a crest.

At the base of the pole is a figure representing Reflections in the Water. This crest is derived from a legend that tells how a woman, crossing a lake on a raft, saw the faces of children in the water. Other members of the family also saw the same faces, and they composed a dirge to commemorate the adoption of the reflections (or shadows) as a crest.

6 ft.
1.8 m

48 LOCATION: *Victoria—Thunderbird Park*
CARVER: *Not known*
CULTURAL STYLE: *Gitksan (Tsimshian)*

An especially fine pole, this is a replica of a memorial pole that belonged to the chief of the Wolf clan of Kitwancool, a village on the Upper Skeena River.

In 1958 the Kitwancool village chiefs allowed several of the old poles to be removed to museums for preservation, on condition that they be replaced with carved replicas and that their histories, territories and laws be written down, published, and made available for teaching purposes. This was accomplished.

A second replica of one of these poles was carved for Thunderbird Park. The original of this pole now stands in the Great Hall of the Museum of Anthropology in Vancouver. At the top is Giant Woodpecker, a crest that originated with the story of an ancestress who kept a Woodpecker as a pet, hiding it in a pit under the house. She fed it constantly until it grew into a huge monster, in the form of a caterpillarlike grub. It tunnelled underground, going from house to house eating up everything made of wood, until it was finally killed. Thus, the family took Woodpecker for a crest.

Below Woodpecker is Mountain Eagle (the equivalent of Thunderbird), who had a craving for human flesh. He kidnapped and mated with a young woman, whose offspring, part bird and part human, he devoured. Eleven children are depicted in two rows, one above and one below Mountain Eagle; notice their varying expressions, arm positions and headgear.

At the base of the pole is Person with a Large Nose, holding a human (perhaps a child) sucking its fingers. The nose of the original was probably long and sharp edged (as on other such figures), carved from a section of wood added to the pole, but the replica does not include this feature.

49 LOCATION: *Victoria—Thunderbird Park*
CARVER: *Mungo Martin with Henry Hunt*
CULTURAL STYLE: *Haida*

This bold and dramatic mortuary pole is a fine example of Haida art. The original, which once stood at Tanu on the Queen Charlotte Islands, was erected for a high-ranking woman who was shot while travelling through the San Juan Islands in Washington. Her body was cremated; the remains were taken back to Tanu and placed in the cavity behind the frontal board.

By 1911 Tanu had been abandoned some years, and Dr. Charles F. Newcombe of Victoria obtained the mortuary pole for the provincial museum, which makes it almost the only such pole that has been preserved. It stood outside the museum until it became evident that continued weathering and rot would eventually cause its destruction.

At that time, the 1950s, with the lack of Haida carvers experienced in creating poles, the task of duplicating it fell to Mungo Martin, a Kwakiutl. Working from the original, he carved a replica of the old Haida pole.

Perched atop the pole is Eagle—the original had a copper (not present in the replica) leaning against its chest. The frontal board represents the mythical Mountain Hawk, with its recurved beak and wings at each side.

Below is Whale, represented only by its head and tail flukes, the latter wrapping part way around the pole on each side. A small figure with three skils (possibly the deceased?) crouches between the ears of Beaver at the base.

The original mortuary pole in the deserted and overgrown village of Tanu, 1901. PHOTOGRAPH BY CHARLES NEWCOMBE, COURTESY ROYAL BRITISH COLUMBIA MUSEUM, PN 100

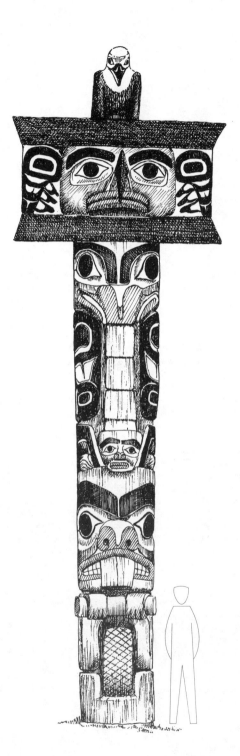

111

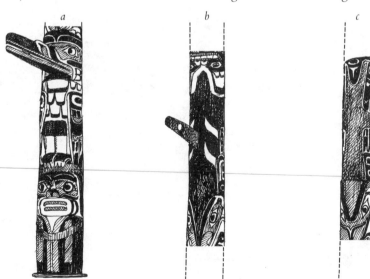

50 LOCATION: *Victoria—Beacon Hill Park, Dallas Rd.*
CARVER: *Mungo Martin with Henry Hunt, David Martin*
CULTURAL STYLE: *Kwakiutl*

Soaring upward from a grassy field is a pole that, for many years, Victoria boasted was the tallest totem pole in the world—until Alert Bay laid claim to the title. Such extremely tall poles are not traditional and would have been impossible to raise in earlier times; now modern technology lends a mechanical hand. This exceptionally tall pole of 38.9 m (127 feet, 7 inches) originated as a publicity stunt organized by the Victoria *Times* newspaper, which gave extensive coverage to the progress of the pole and its raising on 2 July 1956.

Carved by the renowned Mungo Martin, the pole depicts an ancient legend that tells of the origin of a clan of the Kwakiutl people to which he belonged and how it acquired the right to use certain crest figures. Geeksen was one of the "First Men" of the Kwakiutl—human beings who were created in various ways in diverse places and who founded the different clans.

Geeksen lived alone in a small house on the beach, near the mouth of the Nah-witti River at the north end of Vancouver Island. One morning before dawn, he awoke to strange sounds: first the cry of the Hokw-hokw, then the squeal of the Whale, next the Sea Lion's bellow and the Eagle's screech. Peering outside, Geek-

6 ft./1.8 m

112

sen saw a strange sight. Rising out of the beach, growing ever taller, was a pole with live animals and birds on it, one above the other, each adding its voice to the din. At the base, a man wearing a red cedar bark neck ring spoke to Geeksen: "Observe carefully all the figures on the pole. These will be your crests, to be displayed by you and your descendants." Then the pole disappeared.

Now rich in crests and ceremonial property, Geeksen took part in a great gathering of other Kwakiutl clans and founded the Geeksen clan, which has used the crest figures in various ways ever since.

Mungo Martin's tall pole was the first time all the clan's crests had been brought together in one carving. Then, with space on the log left over, he added two First Men from other Kwakiutl stories at the top.

Because of the pole's height, it is difficult to distinguish and identify each crest, but starting at the bottom should make this easier. At the base is Geeksen himself, wearing a ceremonial blanket and cedar bark head ring. Progressing upwards are Hokw-hokw, Killer Whale, Sea Lion, Eagle, Sea Otter (clutching a fish), Whale with an upside-down human, Beaver, Man, Seal, Wolf and finally three men on top of each other, the top two wearing blankets.

This pole received its third coat of paint in August 1989. Working from a massive scaffold, it took two artists several weeks to complete the task.

An undated plaque on the metal base reads: "This tablet in memory of the British Columbia Indians who gave their lives in the World Wars 1914–1918 1939–1945 was erected by the B.C. Indian Arts and Welfare Society."

Part of the scaffolding required for the repainting of the 38-m (127-foot) pole on Beacon Hill in Victoria, 1989.
PHOTOGRAPH BY HILARY STEWART

113

BACKGROUND TO THE "CITY OF TOTEM POLES"

DUNCAN

Duncan, a small town 64 km (40 miles) north of Victoria on Vancouver Island, completed a revitalization project in 1983. Concrete pavers, hanging flower baskets and colourful banners spruced up the town considerably, but they were not enough to prevent tourists from driving through without stopping—until Mayor Douglas Baker hit on an imaginative idea: make Duncan the "City of Totem Poles."

The project began with two Cowichan carvers from the region, Tom and Douglas LaFortune; then a third, Francis Horne, joined them. Twelve large cedar logs were donated by a logging company, and the poles began to take shape in a warehouse type of building, visible from the highway. Enthusiasm mounted, particularly when a Maori carver from Duncan's sister city of Kaikohe in New Zealand came to Duncan to carve a Maori pole. Tupari Te Whata returned to New Zealand with a Northwest Coast Indian totem pole, while his Maori pole remained in Duncan.

By 1986 a series of carved and painted poles, sponsored by local business and industry, lined both sides of the highway through the city, and more poles stood elsewhere. A plaque on an Eagle and Beaver pole reads: "Dedicated to the Mayor and council for his initiative and creation of 'the City of Totem Poles.'"

Duncan surely deserves its title, as with each succeeding year more poles are raised throughout the town. The following is a small selection of those poles. It should be noted, however, that several other poles around town do not hold to the traditional art styles of the cultures that they represent.

LOCATION: *Duncan—on the Island Highway*
CARVER: *Doug LaFortune/Francis Horne*
CULTURAL STYLE: *Kwakiutl*

Two of the many poles on pedestals that line both sides of the main highway that heads up island through Duncan are shown here.

Although the carvers of these two are Coast Salish people, they chose to work in a general Northwest Coast style, combining Kwakiutl with northern design characteristics, and using the traditional red and black colours for feature emphasis. Created by different carvers, the poles were raised in 1986.

Left: This pole by Doug LaFortune is a strong Bear clutching its cub. This sturdy pole, 4.4 m (13 feet, 4 inches) in height, could serve as a house post, with the beam resting in the space between Bear's ears. Large nostrils and big teeth with canines characterize Bear, as do the clawed feet.

Right: A human sits crouched on top of the turned-back tail flukes of Whale, who has a dorsal fin protruding above its head. Another human, kneeling at the base, holds a copper. This pole, 5 m (14 feet, 8 inches) tall, was carved by Francis Horne.

115

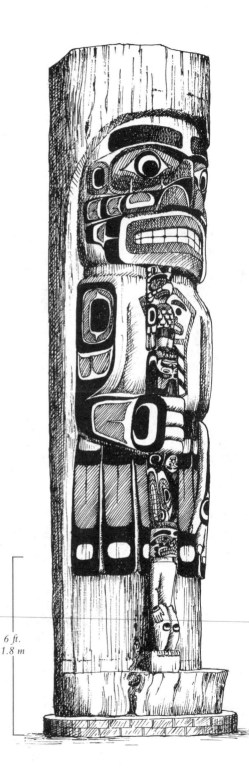

6 ft.
1.8 m

53 LOCATION: *Duncan—Provincial Building, Station St. and Jubilee St.*
CARVER: *Richard Hunt*
CULTURAL STYLE: *Kwakiutl*

Around the time that Genghis Khan was roaming Asia, a cedar seedling sprouted in the fertile soil on the west coast of what we now call Vancouver Island. It grew tall and straight for some 775 years, until Wayne Beecroft, a log merchandising superintendent, came across it near Port Renfrew. For three months he had been on the lookout for a particularly large cedar that the MacMillan Bloedel Company would donate to Duncan's "City of Totem Poles" project.

The diameter of the log, cut well above the flaring base of the tree, measured nearly 2 m (over 6 feet) at the butt. It contained enough wood to roof three two-bedroom houses with cedar shakes.

Richard Hunt was approached about creating a totem pole from the giant cedar. "I was really excited at the chance to work on something so huge," he said, "and I thought about how I could use the log to its fullest width. I decided to carve Cedar Man, the spirit of the cedar tree personified. For inspiration, I used the Cedar Man figure on Mungo Martin's memorial pole in Alert Bay, that my grandfather carved."

The log was delivered to the front of the Provincial Building. For shelter, a huge tent was set up over the enormous tree trunk, and sets of three-tiered bleachers gave the carver access to the sides and top of the log. Many Duncan residents visited regularly, using the bleachers to sit comfortably and watch the pole take shape. To carve such an enormous figure necessitated extra-large tools, and Richard Hunt used double-bit axes, shipwright's adzes and chisels with blades of 9 cm (3½ inches) for much of the work.

Just prior to working on this carving, Richard had made a mask with eyes measuring 2.5 cm (1 inch) across. By comparison, the eyes he carved on Cedar Man were over 40.6 cm (16 inches) across; the head alone measured 1.8 m (6 feet) high, and the talking stick a staggering 4.3 m (14 feet).

Raising the pole by the traditional manner was out of the question because of its size, and a special crane had to be brought in to handle the task. With the pole already raised in place, the ceremonial dedication ceremonies took place on 17 November 1988, and members of the Hunt family, in full regalia, performed traditional dances.

"Seen from a distance," the carver said, "Cedar Man appears to stare down the street at you. He is transforming, walking out of the log." He wears a cedar bark skirt, has a copper painted on his chest and carries a talking stick with Kolus at the top. The mythical bird is followed by Whale, whose turned-back tail flukes are above Cedar Man's large hand, with its head below. At the base of the talking stick is a chief wearing a cedar bark head ring.

This pole's diameter holds the world's record—with little likelihood of its ever being beaten.

6 ft.
1.8 m

Duncan's heritage railway station now houses the Cowichan Valley Museum. Two of the four poles on the south side of the old station are illustrated here.

The pole on the left, by Francis Horne, is topped by an interesting depiction of Owl. The carving shows Owl with its head swivelled to one side—a movement typical of owls—and with a decoratively feathered breast. Beneath is Bear holding a human.

The right-hand pole is by Richard Hunt. His massive Bear figure holds a seal, whose flippers are hidden beneath Bear's great paws and whose tail is turned up from the base. Crouched between Bear's ears is a small creature reminiscent of a frog, though it is without front or hind legs. "It would have been a frog," the carver said, "but the lack of funding for additional carving time resulted in a pollywog."

56 LOCATION: *Nanaimo—north end of Pearson Bridge, at Stewart Ave. and Terminal Ave., "Route of the Totems"*
CARVER: *Jimmy John with his son Norman John*
CULTURAL STYLE: *Nuu-chah-nulth*

Jimmy John, whose original home was Yuquot (now generally known as Friendly Cove), on Vancouver Island, was quite elderly when he carved this dramatic pole in 1966. Born before births were recorded, he was a direct descendant of the renowned Chief Maquinna who met Captain Cook at Friendly Cove in 1778.

Jimmy John was one of fifty-two people who survived a smallpox epidemic that felled a great many of his people in the 1870s. Carving since the age of eighteen years, he created masks, headdresses, feast bowls and other items, including a fine totem pole that still stands at Yuquot. He also carved a pole that was presented to Queen Elizabeth, and he carved a crucifix, from a single piece of wood, that was sent to Pope John XXIII. Nuu-chah-nulth carver Tim Paul described him as "a real powerhouse."

When Jimmy John died in 1987, he was thought to be about 114 years old. His grandson, Sam Johnson Jr., said that the elder had been baptized in 1876 when he was a small boy.

This pole typifies the elderly carver's fluid, flamboyant style, which gives his work a lively appearance. Ellen White of the Nanaimo Band said it was she who provided Jimmy John with the story that he depicted on the pole. The story tells of a time long ago when her people, who relied largely on shellfish, found themselves short of food. They had not realized that there were fish in the river, until one day an Eagle swooped over the water and picked up a salmon in its strong claws. Eventually the people came to depend on the salmon in the river, smoking and drying it for winter. Like the Eagle, the Bear harvested salmon from the streams, and chiefs reminded the men to show the strength of the Bear in order to supply winter food for all the village, including the old and the feeble.

Thus, Jimmy John's pole carries Eagle at the top, looking down onto Bear, who has a salmon in its mouth and paws. The head on Bear's chest represents the guardian, or master, of the ceremonial dance house.

6 ft.
1.8 m

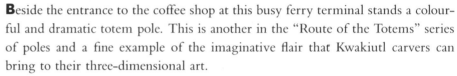

57 LOCATION: *Departure Bay—Nanaimo Ferry Terminal, "Route of the Totems"*
CARVER: *Kwakiutl Arts and Crafts Organization*
CULTURAL STYLE: *Kwakiutl*

Beside the entrance to the coffee shop at this busy ferry terminal stands a colourful and dramatic totem pole. This is another in the "Route of the Totems" series of poles and a fine example of the imaginative flair that Kwakiutl carvers can bring to their three-dimensional art.

With outspread and uplifted wings, the great Thunderbird appears ready to take flight as it glares down at passers-by. Below is Bear eating a salmon held in its paws, the strong muscles of its front legs indicated by painted designs.

6 ft.
1.8 m

58 LOCATION: *Qualicum Beach—on the Island Highway, "Route of the Totems"*
CARVER: *Simon Charlie*
CULTURAL STYLE: *Coast Salish*

6 ft.
1.8 m

This unusual pole, a favourite of many, combines the three-dimensional realism of the Coast Salish tradition with the carver's personal style. After the cedar log for this "Route of the Totems" pole was delivered to his house, Simon Charlie checked on local history to find an appropriate subject to go with the required Grizzly Bear, but without success. "I sat on the log for three days wondering what to carve," he said, "then I thought about the name Qualicum—it means dog-salmon in our language."

One morning Simon came out of his house and found blood on one end of the log. This ill omen troubled him deeply. "I decided to fight that," he said. "I used my mind to fight it." He succeeded. When the pole was finished, it won a special prize for originality.

Simon Charlie chose a golden eagle for the top figure and carved a dog-salmon in its claws. As a carver of the traditional (and only) Coast Salish mask, the Swaixwhe, he has portrayed this on the Grizzly Bear's chest. Because his people believe that any major bird or animal body part that moves has its own spirit, he added faces to the soles of the bear's feet. "Life always has a happy side as well as a sad side, you know. So I made one face happy and the other one sad," he said.

The sculpture is finished with the adzing texture that is a trademark of his work, and in this instance it gives the impression of fur.

59 LOCATION: *Courtenay—Tourist Infocentre, "Route of the Totems"*
CARVER: *Kwakiutl Arts and Crafts Organization*
CULTURAL STYLE: *Kwakiutl*

6 ft.
1.8 m

This fine pole, which is on the Island Highway at the south entrance to Courtenay, won second prize in the "Route of the Totems" series contest.

The imposing and elaborately painted bird at the top is Kolus, younger brother of Thunderbird. On his chest is incorporated the mystic Hwhy-Hwhy mask of the nearby Comox people. The origins of this mask lie in an encounter by their ancestors who, while travelling through a swampy area of the upper Quinsam River (near Campbell River), saw two strange figures moving through the rising mists. Believing them to be the figures of a spirit man and woman, the travellers returned home, where carvers depicted the likeness of the spirit people.

Beneath is Grizzly Bear, holding Dzoonokwa, whose baby was discovered by a young man in its cradle in the forest. He teased the baby by pinching its toe, causing it to cry loudly. Dzoonokwa, who was a short distance away, heard the cry and called out, "Whoever you are that may be teasing my baby, let him alone and I will give you a spear."

Pleased at such good fortune, the young man pinched the baby on three more occasions, with the result that he was offered the Water of Life, a magic wand and a supernatural canoe if he would leave the baby alone. Satisfied, the man stopped teasing the child, returned home with his gifts and, because of his encounter with Dzoonokwa, became rich and powerful.

An old story tells of two brothers who felled a cedar and carved a dugout canoe. The younger brother insisted on launching the craft even though it was not finished and the paddles were not yet made. He had, however, painted a double-headed sea serpent on the sides of the canoe. Putting his older brother in the bow, facing forward, the younger brother sang a special power song and slapped his hands alongside the stern, where he sat, causing the canoe to propel itself through the water with great speed.

60 LOCATION: *Courtenay—Lewis Park*
CARVER: *Mungo Martin with David Martin, Henry Hunt*
CULTURAL STYLE: *Kwakiutl*

6 ft.
1.8 m

An interesting background comes with the pair of poles at the entrance to Lewis Park. In 1927 the Courtenay Board of Trade acquired two poles said to have been carved by Johnny Tla-kwa-dzi, a carver from Salmon River. However, local historian George Pidcock said the poles belonged to Chief Joe Wallace, who carved them at Cape Mudge for the entrance to his house but who reached old age and blindness before acquiring the necessary wealth to raise them.

Over the years, the poles became badly decayed. The British Columbia Provincial Museum arranged for two new poles to be carved by Mungo Martin, with assistance from his son David and the notable young carver Henry Hunt, at a cost of $1,000. Whether he replicated the originals or carved his own version of the same figures is not known, but Mungo, being a master carver, likely created his own version of the same figures.

In 1957 the newly carved and freshly painted poles were raised in a traditional ceremony attended by many high-ranking native people, resplendent in ceremonial regalia. Ancient songs and dances were performed in front of a dance screen, giving Chief Andy Frank of Comox, who organized the event, the opportunity to wear a special mask—the Swaixwhe—for only the second time in his life. He had received it in 1927, on the occasion of his marriage in a native ceremony.

Although the poles were raised by crane, there was initially a demonstration of the old method of pole raising. As a wealth token, Chief Andy Frank placed a silver dollar under the base of each pole; he also gave quantities of silver dollars to those who had assisted in the whole event, and he gave gas money to those who had travelled to attend. In addition, many visiting natives and representatives of pioneer families were his guests at a banquet at a restaurant in Courtenay.

The two poles differ slightly; the one illustrated is on the left of the park entrance. Chief Andy Frank's wife, Margaret, spoke of the pole in her native language, translated for me by her daughter Mary Everson. (Margaret Frank played the part of Naida, the young heroine in Edward Curtis's feature film in 1914—and remembers it well.) At the top is Thunderbird, wings outspread; beneath is Sisiutl, whose two heads and their tongues appear as a single head with a split tongue. At the base is the upper portion of a copper with a whale design.

123

6 ft.
1.8 m

61 LOCATION: *Comox Reserve—on Dyke Rd. between Courtenay and Comox*
CARVER: *Calvin Hunt*
CULTURAL STYLE: *Kwakiutl*

Between Courtenay and Comox lies the Comox Reserve, where Mary Clifton was born in a traditional Kwakiutl plank house in 1900, and in front of the house stood an old welcome pole. She recalled that on it was the carved figure of a man, one hand shading his eyes, looking out over the shore, with the other hand reaching out in a welcoming gesture.

As a small child, Mary accompanied her mother and others from the village to a fish cannery at Quathiaski Cove on Quadra Island, where they were seasonally employed each summer. "In those days," she said, "we went by canoe"—a journey of some 64 km (40 miles). "One year, when we got home, that welcome pole had been stolen," Mary said, adding wistfully, "but in those days there was nothing you could do about it."

When plans were being made to raise a memorial pole in honour of her brother, Chief Andy Frank, Mary, nearly ninety years old, suggested that the pole should have on it the welcome figure of the old Frank home. As a child, Calvin Hunt had known Andy Frank and recalled that "He always had a smile on his face. I felt honoured to be asked to create the memorial for this great man." Working in his Fort Rupert studio near Port Hardy, he topped the pole with the old figure—one hand in the welcome gesture, the other holding a copper to symbolize Andy Frank's chiefly position. Beneath, he carved Whale, the main crest of this high-ranking and much-loved man who died in 1972.

An ancient legend tells of two brothers who, knowing that a flood was coming, went up the valley and each made a canoe. The waters rose, and when all the land was covered, a Whale surfaced near them; they tied their canoes to it until the waters receded, and they eventually became the founders of the Comox and the Puntledge people. The Whale, it is said, can still be seen on the mountain.

The memorial pole was raised in front of the reserve's Ceremonial Big House (originally built by Chief Andy Frank and recently renovated by Calvin Hunt) on 20 May 1989. A large crowd, including many people from distant places, gathered for the ceremony and the attendant potlatch inside the spacious building. Two dramatic Thunderbird house posts, with a painted screen between, formed a backdrop for the many drummers beating on the long log drum, carved and

Carver Calvin Hunt (right) *holds one of the two front lines that prevent his pole from swaying as it is raised in Comox, 1989. The use of block and tackle is a practical compromise between hand hauling and mechanical means. After the pole is upright, Whale's dorsal fin will be added.*
PHOTOGRAPH BY HILARY STEWART

painted in the form of Whale by Calvin. Smoke from the central fire rose up through the smoke hole all afternoon and evening as a series of dancers, ceremonially robed or wearing elaborately carved masks, performed their special dances. The eight-hour event, with speeches and tributes (mainly in the Kwakwala language) to Chief Andy Frank, a sumptuous feast for over five hundred people and the giving of money to everyone present, affirmed the status of this past chief of the Comox Band.

This major event, held on the reserve and right beside the highway, made a proud statement and was in bold contrast to the earlier time when both the house and the memorial pole were tucked away in a city park.

6 ft.
1.8 m

62 LOCATION: *Comox Reserve—on Dyke Rd. between Courtenay and Comox*
CARVER: *Mungo Martin*
CULTURAL STYLE: *Kwakiutl*

Easily noticed from the road is the Comox Reserve's Ceremonial Big House, its front painted with Thunderbird grasping a huge Whale in its claws. Standing before it, to the left, is a memorial pole by master carver Mungo Martin. Both the house and this pole have a touching history.

The Big House was originally constructed in 1958, only the second on the coast to be built since early times—the other being at Thunderbird Park in Victoria. But in those days there was a lack of pride in being Indian, and to conceal their reserve from the general populace, the band located the Big House in Centennial Park, just outside nearby Courtenay.

Mungo Martin's son David had carved three of the house posts inside. A year later, on board a salmon seiner that was crossing from Comox to Steveston, he was swept overboard in heavy seas. Despite an intensive search, his body was never found. The death of his only son was devastating to Mungo Martin, and one year later, following tradition, he raised a memorial pole in his son's honour. Then eighty-two years old, he carved the pole entirely alone. It was raised in a sad and solemn ceremony beside the Big House in Centennial Park, on 26 May 1960.

In 1974, with a renewed sense of pride and identity spreading among native people everywhere, and to fulfil a wish by the late Chief Andy Frank, the Comox Band moved both the house and the pole to take their rightful place on the reserve. It is there that the pole now stands in memory of a man who would have inherited all his father's crests, rights and privileges.

At the top is Hokw-hokw with the Sun crest below; the high-ranking man at the base—notice the head and neck rings—represents the chiefly lineage to which David Martin belonged. A marble tablet in front of the pole reads simply: "DAVID MARTIN July 1 1917–Sept 4 1959 KWAKIUTL TRIBE."

126

63 LOCATION: *Campbell River—Coast Discovery Inn, south end of Tyee Plaza Shopping Mall*
CARVER: *Sam Henderson*
CULTURAL STYLE: *Kwakiutl*

The expansion of tourism in Campbell River—dubbed "The Salmon Capital of the World"—brought a new and attractive hotel overlooking the salmon-rich waters of Discovery Passage. The owners of the Coast Discovery Inn, built in 1965, commissioned the renowned Campbell River carver Sam Henderson to create a totem pole to enhance the new building's exterior.

Henderson remembered the fine pole that had once stood on his reserve and that had belonged to his wife's father's family, the Kwasistala (sometimes spelled Quocksister) family. In 1910 they had been persuaded by a New York collector to sell the pole to a museum there, and so Henderson decided to make a new version of the old pole. When he had married his wife, May—in both traditional native and non-native ceremonies—the couple acquired each other's crests. This gave him the right to carve his wife's family pole, which was raised and dedicated on 9 June 1965. Eighteen years later, a year after Henderson's death, his son, Mark, also an artist and carver, gave his father's work a new coat of paint.

Although the original pole was topped by a Thunderbird, Sam Henderson chose to make his top figure Eagle. Below are Whale, Raven and Bear.

6 ft.
1.8 m

127

64 LOCATION: *Campbell River—Coast Discovery Inn, south end of Tyee Plaza Shopping Mall*
CARVER: *Sam Henderson*
CULTURAL STYLE: *Kwakiutl*

Also commissioned by the Coast Discovery Inn, this pole is another by the renowned local carver Sam Henderson. Born in 1905, he clung to and nurtured Kwakiutl Indian traditions throughout his life, passing them on to his family and, later, other younger generations.

Sam Henderson was deeply knowledgeable in the roles and rights that dictated the potlatch. Fluent in his native tongue, he was also a dancer, composer, singer and speaker until his death in 1982.

Thunderbird tops this totem pole, raised in 1965, followed beneath by Whale and a human at the base.

6 ft.
1.8 m

65 LOCATION: *Campbell River—Tyee Plaza Shopping Mall*
CARVER: *Sam Henderson*
CULTURAL STYLE: *Kwakiutl*

For several years in the early 1970s, the Tyee Plaza Merchants Association had been staging an annual marketing device and tourist attraction that they called "Pow-Wow Days." Sales clerks dressed up in fake Plains Indian costumes, and Rose McKay, curator of the town's museum, loaned items from the museum collection for display in store windows.

Elizabeth Kwasistala, a Kwakiutl woman of the nearby Campbell River Reserve, objected to the word "pow-wow" (a word originating with the Algonquin Indians of eastern Canada, and referring to a gathering or conference). She suggested instead "Bakuum Days," the word in her language meaning native people, as opposed to *mamalha*, white people.

To give local native authenticity to the event, Rose McKay suggested that a memorial pole be raised in honour of her good friend Pete Smith, a Kwakiutl elder from Tourner Island. The Tyee Plaza Merchants Association liked the idea and commissioned Sam Henderson to carve the pole. The right to use Dzoonokwa had been passed to Pete Smith's family in a potlatch, and for the memorial Henderson carved Dzoonokwa holding a copper in her hands.

On 23 May 1975 the colourful pole-raising ceremony, with native drumming, dancing and speech making, brought the true flavour and dignity of Northwest Coast Indian culture to the plaza, dispelling the earlier stereotyped Indian image.

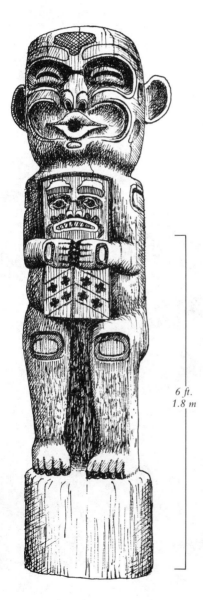

6 ft.
1.8 m

129

66/67 LOCATION: *Campbell River—Foreshore Park*
CARVER: *Various*
CULTURAL STYLE: *Kwakiutl*

6 ft.
1.8 m

Standing at the water's edge, looking across Discovery Passage to Quadra Island, Heritage Pavilion in Foreshore Park takes the form of the framework of a traditional Kwakiutl-style house. One pair of carved house posts at either end supports crossbeams, which in turn carry the main roof beams. An early village would have had a long row, sometimes two, of similarly constructed houses facing the water.

The pair of house posts at the eastern end, towards the sea, was created by Bob Neel, son of the famed carver Ellen Neel (1916–1966), with the assistance of Eugene Alfred Sr. and Dora Sewid Cook. Beneath the Eagles with outstretched wings are humans holding salmon.

The two house posts at the opposite end, and both the crosspieces with carvings of Sisiutl, were the work of the renowned Campbell River carver Sam Henderson (1905–1982) and his sons Bill and Ernie. The figures represent crests that belong to the family, handed down through many generations and acquired through the potlatch system.

Notice the two massive roof beams, decoratively adzed, each an 18.3-m (60-foot) clear cedar log from the Nimpkish Valley, one of the oldest stands of timber on northern Vancouver Island. Also notice the dugout canoe hanging under the roof peak—a gift of the native people of Church House, a village at the entrance to Bute Inlet.

The beginning of the 1973 Campbell River Annual Salmon Festival saw the dedication of Heritage Pavilion, with an elaborate ceremony that involved members of native bands from Campbell River, Cape Mudge and Alert Bay. The festival committee produced a 35-minute sound and colour film showing the construction of the pavilion, with Dora Sewid Cook, one of the carvers, narrating some of the history of her people.

Katie Henderson McKay and Bill Glendale (holding a carved rattle) dance at the dedication ceremony of the Heritage Pavilion in Campbell River, 1973. COURTESY CAMPBELL RIVER MUSEUM AND ARCHIVES, COURIER–UPPER ISLAND COLLECTION

6 ft.
1.8 m

LOCATION: *Campbell River—Campbell River Museum and Archives, "Route of the Totems"*
CARVER: *Sam Henderson*
CULTURAL STYLE: *Kwakiutl*

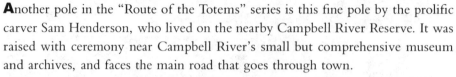

Another pole in the "Route of the Totems" series is this fine pole by the prolific carver Sam Henderson, who lived on the nearby Campbell River Reserve. It was raised with ceremony near Campbell River's small but comprehensive museum and archives, and faces the main road that goes through town.

The carver created a big, bold Eagle, typically Kwakiutl in style, with outspread wings painted in a strong design; a head with face painting decorates Eagle's chest. Below is an equally powerful rendering of Grizzly Bear, who holds a human figure. The entire pole is painted in red, black and white.

6 ft.
1.8 m

69 LOCATION: *Campbell River—Thunderbird Hall, 1400 We-Wai-Kum Rd.,*
Campbell River Reserve
CARVER: *Bill Henderson with Sam Henderson Jr., Patrick Hunt*
CULTURAL STYLE: *Kwakiutl*

Fronting the We-Wai-Kum Band's large, modern community hall stands a tall pole—a memorial to Chief Bill Roberts, a renowned chief of the band for many years. Both the height and location of this memorial pole carry significance.

A successful fisherman in his day, Bill Roberts always liked to have his trolling poles "exactly 42 feet long" (12.8 m), and so it seemed appropriate to remember him with a carved memorial pole of that length. "When I carved the miniature pole for the Roberts family's approval, before tackling the large version," Bill Henderson said, "I made it 42 inches" (106.7 cm).

Bill Roberts was a strong and determined individual who involved himself in political issues. As a youth, he had served in World War II in England. As a chief of his people, he was active in such organizations as the Native Brotherhood and the United Native Nations. "He was always going to meetings" the carver recalls. "He was instrumental in getting us this community hall and in getting the band's marina going."

The chief's memorial, raised in June 1986, now graces the front of that hall, and at the band's cemetery, a headstone marking his burial reads: "In loving memory of Chief William Roberts whose family held the highest rank among his people. Always remembered for his devotion to better the Indian's way of life."

The figures on the pole illustrate a legend belonging to the Roberts family. It concerns a Whale stuck in rocks at Gowlland Harbour (on Quadra Island, across from the village), a big man with a copper and Kolus, who lifted the Whale out. The mythical Kolus, with elaborately painted wings, graces the top of this memorial pole. Below is Whale, with long pectoral fins and a turned-back tail having a face, followed by Sun, a crest of the Roberts family. At the base is the big man with the copper.

133

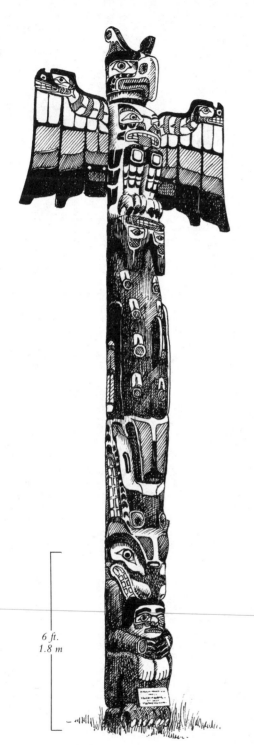

6 ft.
1.8 m

70 LOCATION: *Campbell River—We-Wai-Kum Band cemetery, Campbell River Reserve*
CARVER: *Ernie Henderson with Bill Henderson*
CULTURAL STYLE: *Kwakiutl*

Standing out against the sky and distant islands, and surrounded by gravestones, are two memorial poles in the cemetery of the We-Wai-Kum Band. The one on the left is a memorial to the renowned carver and greatly esteemed chief of high rank, Sam Henderson. Not only was he a carver, with major works in key public locations and museums, he was also a protector of ancient Kwakiutl traditions.

Sam Henderson died in 1982 at the age of 77 years. Seventeen months later, a memorial pole carved by two of his sons, Ernie and Bill, was raised with difficulty against a wind blowing in from the sea. The following day, when the pole was unveiled in solemn ceremony before a very large crowd, the wind abated.

At the pole's top, wings outstretched, is Eagle, the carver's main crest inherited from his mother. Beneath Eagle is the central head of Sisiutl, its scaly, snakelike body folded in half down the pole, terminating in two heads whose tongues meet in the centre. The supernatural Sisiutl had the power to help as well as to harm. If a canoe at sea was unable to proceed because of wind, Sisiutl would surface and fold itself in half to form a canoe; the paddlers would transfer to its safety, towing their own canoe behind the self-propelled serpent.

At the base of the pole stands Dzoonokwa holding her child. To the right of the memorial pole, a gravestone carries the inscription: "Samuel Henderson, Snr., May 21–1905 — Nov. 20–1982. He lives in our hearts forever." There are only a few instances where a person has both a headstone and a memorial pole, but Sam and May Henderson each have both.

71 LOCATION: *Campbell River—We-Wai-Kum Band, Campbell River Reserve*
CARVER: *Sam Henderson*
CULTURAL STYLE: *Kwakiutl*

The memorial pole standing next to Sam Henderson's is that of his beloved wife May, the eldest daughter of the high-ranking Capt. John Quocksister (Kwasistala) of Campbell River. A strong and influential woman, she was highly revered for her role both in the community at large and within the band. To the right of her pole, a headstone reads simply: "Mother, May Louise Henderson. Mar. 17/1917–Sept. 17/ 1978." The word "mother" carries significance for a woman who bore seven sons and eight daughters.

The memorial displays May Henderson's crests. At the top is Thunderbird, with an interesting design device: Sisiutl, stretched across the top edge of Thunderbird's outspread wings, has its central head on the bird's chest. Beneath is a large Grey Whale, head down, with its tail flukes curved over its back. The short dorsal and long pectoral fins identify the sea mammal. At the base is Bear holding a child.

Traditionally, totem poles always faced the water, the route of travel for anyone arriving at the village. But these poles, in a different time and context, face not the sea but the contemporary route of travel—the roadway.

135

6 ft.
1.8 m

72 LOCATION: *Cape Mudge, Quadra Island—Kwagiulth Museum and Cultural Centre*
CARVER: *Dora Sewid Cook with Eugene Alfred Sr. and Jeff Wallace*
CULTURAL STYLE: *Kwakiutl*

This pole is a recarving of one of three welcome figures that were given by Chief Wakius of Alert Bay to Major Dick of Cape Mudge as part of a dowry. They stood inside his big house at Cape Mudge until his death, when they were moved to his gravehouse on the foreshore. Many years of outdoor exposure caused their deterioration before the Campbell River and District Museum collected and preserved two of the poles, the third being too rotted to save.

In 1972 the Cape Mudge Band brought together several petroglyph boulders endangered by erosion and created Petroglyph Park (across the road from the museum). Dora Sewid Cook and assistants carved three new figures that stood to welcome people to the park, but in 1979, with the opening of the Kwagiulth Museum in the village, the poles were moved to welcome visitors there. The Campbell River museum returned the two original figures, which are now housed in the Kwagiulth Museum.

When Chief Wakius gave the original carvings to Major Dick, this story (told in brief form here) was given with them:

Paddling upriver, a man and his servant reached a village occupied only by an old blind woman and her granddaughter. When the man ordered his servant to fetch water from the river, the old woman warned him of a huge river monster, which had swallowed all the villagers who had gone near the water. The man took off his belt, made in the form of a Sisiutl, and put it around his servant for protection, but to no avail, for the river monster swallowed him. The man called to the Sisiutl, "Break apart! Break apart!" The monster jumped ashore and his stomach broke apart, releasing the servant, human bones and others still half-alive. The man splashed the Water of Life on them, and they revived; he also splashed it on the blind woman's eyes, and her sight returned.

The Sisiutl around the waist of this welcome figure commemorates the achievements of the supernatural creature and recalls the story that goes with the carving.

136

73 LOCATION: *Cape Mudge, Quadra Island—Kwagiulth Museum and Cultural Centre*
CARVER: *Sam Henderson with Bill Henderson, Ernie Henderson*
CULTURAL STYLE: *Kwakiutl*

6 ft.
1.8 m

The Kwagiulth Museum at Cape Mudge, built in 1979, houses a collection of potlatch ceremonial regalia, all of which had been confiscated by federal government agents during the large and now famous Dan Cranmer potlatch of 1921. After years of negotiations, many of these valuable family heirlooms were finally returned to their owners at Cape Mudge and housed in the museum built especially for the purpose.

Standing boldly beside the front entrance of the attractive building is a totem pole that was originally created for Expo '70 in Osaka, Japan. It was carved by Sam Henderson of Campbell River, with help from his two sons, Bill and Ernie. Placed in front of the museum, it was formally dedicated on 12 November 1980, with a ceremony followed by the customary colourful potlatch and feast.

Thunderbird, with wings folded, tops the pole. This crest was a *kaysoo*, that is, a gift brought to the carver from his wife's lineage, through his marriage to her.

The figure at the base represents the chief or "first man" of the Nakwakto people of Blunden Harbour, Sam Henderson's original home. The chief carries a painted rattle in his hands.

The squarish ovoids painted on the knees of seated figures are generally an identifying mark of Henderson's work.

74 LOCATION: *Alert Bay—Alert Bay cemetery*
CARVER: *Henry Hunt and Tony Hunt*
CULTURAL STYLE: *Kwakiutl*

On a grey day in September 1970, more than a thousand people gathered to pay homage to a man renowned along the coast as a great Kwakiutl chief and for his role in preserving and passing on his people's artistic skills and knowledge, as well as traditional beliefs.

Mungo Martin had died on 16 August 1962, at the age of seventy-eight. His body lay in state in the traditional plank house he had built in Thunderbird park, Victoria; his specially made coffin was carved with his crests at both ends, and a replica of his copper was carved on top. To fulfil his wish to be buried among his people, the casket was taken to Alert Bay on board the naval vessel HMCS *Ottawa*. The coffin was covered with flowers and guarded by four sentries with fixed bay-

Master carver Mungo Martin with two unfinished poles, in the carving shed on the University of British Columbia campus, 1951. COURTESY MUSEUM OF ANTHROPOLOGY, UNIVERSITY OF BRITISH COLUMBIA

138

onets during the voyage north. As the boat left Victoria harbour, every flag dipped in respect.

The elaborately carved totem pole, raised by hand-hauled ropes in the Alert Bay cemetery, stands beside the grave of the widely acclaimed chief. It was the first pole raised in the village in forty years. At the ceremony, many high-ranking chiefs, richly dressed in ceremonial regalia and all speaking their native tongue, testified to the worth and stature of this great man. Four chiefs each spoke about the four carved crests belonging to Mungo. The traditional pageantry was followed by lavish feasting and further ceremonies in the cedar dance house. Carved house posts and a painted screen created a backdrop to the drummers and dancers, as a fire blazed in the centre of the earth floor.

The figure at the top of the memorial pole is Kolus, who founded the lineage from which Mungo's grandfather was descended; he has a copper painted on his chest. Below is Cedar Man emerging from the log, holding a copper and a carved talking stick—both based on those owned by the chief. The third figure is Raven, holding a copper in his beak, wings at his sides. At the base is Dzoonokwa, a crest that Mungo Martin acquired through his marriage to his wife Abaya. The depiction of four coppers on one pole attests to the high rank and prestige of this remarkable man.

An additional memorial to Mungo Martin is a wooden plaque, designed by Bill Reid and carved by Tony Kronings, at the Royal British Columbia Museum. It depicts Mungo Martin both in chiefly attire holding his talking stick and copper, and in working clothes carving a totem pole.

6 ft.
1.8 m

139

75 LOCATION: *Alert Bay—Nimpkish Band cemetery*
CARVER: *Willie Seaweed with Joe Seaweed*
CULTURAL STYLE: *Kwakiutl*

A much-photographed pole is this memorial to Billie Moon. The pole, carved at the village of Ba'a's in Blunden Harbour in 1931, is by Willie Seaweed, a man renowned for his prolific output of exceptionally fine Hamatsa masks. His son, Joe, assisted him.

Blunden Harbour, in its northern isolation, maintained its old customs for longer than other villages on the coast, and Willie Seaweed, born in 1873, continued his people's tradition of well-crafted carving. This is one of his finest creations. He died in 1967.

The finished pole was towed by fishboat from Blunden Harbour to Alert Bay, some 58 km (36 miles) to the south. Since that time, it has been repainted at least twice, resulting in changes to the many design details.

The memorial is topped by Thunderbird, its claws grasping the head of the giantess Dzoonokwa, with her characteristic sleepy eyes, pursed lips and pendent breasts.

6 ft.
1.8 m

Jonathan Hunt was born in Fort Rupert in 1874, in a traditional plank house that was the model for the one inside the Royal British Columbia Museum. He was the grandson of George Hunt, the man with whom the renowned anthropologist Franz Boas worked so closely during more than forty years of documenting the Kwakiutl culture.

Jonathan was also the great-grandfather of Tony Hunt, and he was already quite elderly when he attended the ceremonies in Alert Bay for the raising of Mungo Martin's memorial pole, which Tony and his father had carved. Mungo and Jonathan had been close friends for many years, and during the eulogy that Jonathan gave at the pole raising, he said, looking Tony Hunt in the eye: "When I die, I want a pole just like my best friend's."

A few years later, Jonathan Hunt died at the age of ninety-nine years. His great-grandson fulfilled the elder's wish by carving a memorial pole equal to that of Mungo Martin's. Six days of ceremonies and potlatching accompanied the pole-raising event, which included the transference of hereditary rights and privileges to Hunt family members. "It was at this time," Tony Hunt recalled, "that I began asserting my role as a chief."

The memorial pole has Kolus perched at the top, followed by Cedar Man holding a copper. Beneath is Sun in human form, also holding a copper; at the base is Whale, head downward, with its tail turned back onto its body.

6 ft.
1.8 m

141

77 LOCATION: *Alert Bay—Nimpkish Band cemetery*
CARVER: *Doug Cranmer with Richard Hunt, Bruce Alfred, Donna Ambers, Fah Ambers, Richard Sumner*
CULTURAL STYLE: *Kwakiutl*

The name Dan Cranmer is legendary on the Northwest Coast, particularly among the Kwakiutl. In 1921 when potlatching was illegal, Dan Cranmer gave a potlatch so opulent (gifts included twenty-four canoes, five gas boats and three pool tables) that the lawmakers pounced hard. Thirty-four people were charged; some went to jail, and others surrendered their ceremonial masks and other objects in lieu of a sentence. After a long battle with the federal government, the native people of Alert Bay and Cape Mudge eventually succeeded in having many of these items returned.

Dan Cranmer and his wife had nine children; the first of them to die was his namesake Dan, for whom a fine memorial pole was raised in 1978. It was created by his brother, Doug Cranmer, a renowned carver, who, with several assistants, worked on the pole close to where the museum that now houses the returned potlatch collection was built. Rushed for time to complete the work, Doug finished painting the pole even as it was being carried to the cemetery. Traditional ceremonies in the large dance house and a lavish potlatch accompanied the solemn event of Dan Cranmer's memorial.

The figure at the top is Thunderbird (wings now fallen off), standing on the centre head of Sisiutl, with a man holding a spear between the body of the two-headed serpent. Below is Killer Whale, its head downward. At the base is Giant Halibut, a mythical being who, at the mouth of the Nimpkish River, shed his tail, fins and skin, transformed into a human, and became the founder of the Nimpkish people.

78 LOCATION: *Port Hardy—Port Hardy Ferry Terminal, "Route of the Totems"*
CARVER: *Henry Hunt*
CULTURAL STYLE: *Kwakiutl*

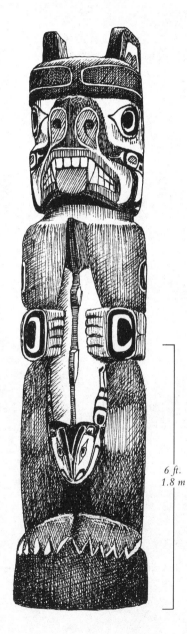

6 ft.
1.8 m

Travellers making the day-long ferry voyage from Port Hardy through the scenically spectacular Inside Passage to Prince Rupert will see a "Route of the Totems" pole close to the pay booths at the entrance to the terminal.

The pole originally stood at the ferry terminal at Kelsey Bay, some 112 km (70 miles) south of its present location, which was as far north as the road went. With the extension of the highway to Port Hardy, the ferry terminal was relocated there in 1979 to shorten the long voyage, and the totem pole went with it.

Carved by Henry Hunt, the pole portrays Grizzly Bear holding a salmon. It is painted all over in red, black and white, colours that harmonize with the grey and reddish tones in the rocky bluff backing it.

143

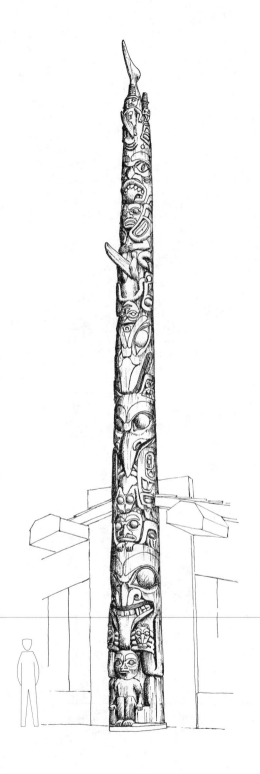

79 LOCATION: *Skidegate—Skidegate Band Council administration building*
CARVER: *Bill Reid with Gary Edenshaw and others*
CULTURAL STYLE: *Haida*

When the Skidegate Band Council needed larger premises, they considered purchasing a double-wide trailer. What they eventually got was an attractive cedar building designed by Rudy Kovacs on the lines of the traditional six-beam plank houses that had once lined the beach in profusion.

Bill Reid, talking one day with Chief Councillor Percy Williams, deplored the lack of poles in the village. There remained only a single, weather-worn, decaying pole out of the dozens that once had stood before the old houses. And thus an idea was born: Reid would design and carve a new pole to front the administration building. Because Haida art had been the focus of his long and successful career, and because his mother had come from Skidegate, he would donate the pole as a tangible expression of his gratitude.

Bill Reid spent the summers of 1976 and 1977 at Second Beach near Skidegate, working under a small plastic-covered framework as shelter against the elements. The 18.3-m (60-foot) log protruded from both ends of the shelter; as each section of carving was completed, the lightweight shelter was moved along to the next uncarved area. Haida carver Gary Edenshaw (now better known as Guu-jaau) made a significant contribution to the work, and well-known artist/carvers such as Robert Davidson, Gerry Marks and Joe David volunteered their carving skills.

Scores of visitors, many from around the world, stopped by to watch as the flying wood chips piled up around the log. Those attending the party at the project's completion went home with autographed chips of red cedar.

On 10 June 1978 the pole was carried, to the beat of drums, along the highway into Skidegate. It was raised with much pomp and ceremony against a background of rich and colourful regalia worn by high-ranking native people from all along the coast. Visitors came from as far away as Ottawa. Fifteen hundred native and non-native people attended the potlatch that evening, at a sit-down feast comprised mainly of a wide assortment of local seafoods. Gifts were distributed to everyone.

The unpainted pole, now weathered to a silver grey, represents the animal kingdom with a fish, a bird, a sea mammal and a land animal. At the top, four Watchmen are grouped around the asymmetrical tail of Shark, with a large

Raising Bill Reid's pole at Skidegate. Willing hands hold two ropes at the front of the pole to prevent it from swaying as it is raised by ropes from behind. A series of crutches helps support the pole's weight. PHOTOGRAPH BY HILARY STEWART

downturned mouth and pointed teeth. Below are the three principals of the Nanasimget story—the husband clasping the tail flukes of Whale, and the wife (upside-down) on its back. Raven, beneath, has Frog in his beak; the human head and hands signify the human side of Raven and form his upturned tail. Grizzly Bear at the base represents the Bear Mother story.

In 1988 a fierce wind sent the single, old, decayed pole crashing to the ground, but Skidegate is not without a cedar monument.

80 LOCATION: *Old Masset—St. John's Church*
CARVER: *Robert Davidson with Reg Davidson*
CULTURAL STYLE: *Haida*

In 1965 a Haida youngster left his native village of Old Masset, on the Queen Charlotte Islands, to attend secondary school in Vancouver. While visiting a museum there, he came to realize the greatness of his artistic heritage. He saw bowls, ladles, boxes, masks and paddles—all carved from wood—as well as miniature totem poles of argillite, a soft black stone found on the islands. He was deeply impressed and began to carve. The youngster was Robert Davidson, now an artist, carver and jeweller of international repute.

At nineteen years old he apprenticed under Bill Reid, and together they carved a 1.8-m (6-foot) totem pole—the master carving one side, the apprentice the other. He also attended the Vancouver School of Art.

On a subsequent visit to Old Masset, the young carver felt a deep compassion for the elders, people out of touch with their once rich and flourishing artistic culture. He "felt driven" to carve a totem pole for them. For inspiration, he turned to old photos of his village and chose a simple-looking pole. Consulting with his eighty-nine-year-old grandfather, Robert showed him a photo of the pole. "I can't see it," the elder said. "Do me a drawing so I can see it."

"So I made a drawing," Robert said, "and I had to create my own interpretations for figures that weren't clear in the old photo."

Claude Davidson, Robert's father, felled a tree for the pole, but it was not big enough for the carver. He felled another, and Robert, only twenty-two years old, set about the formidable task of carving a 16.8-m (40-foot) traditional Haida pole. When it was finally raised, by hand, in the late summer of 1968, with a large crowd to witness and attend a traditional potlatch, it was the first totem pole to be raised in the Queen Charlotte Islands in close to a hundred years.

Three high-hatted Watchmen crouch at the top of this pole, which is composed of three Bears, with several small humans and a Frog between their ears and on their chests. At the pole raising, the carver interpreted the figures as representing the Bear Mother story. Research carried out in later years describes the figures at the base of the old pole (indistinct in the photo) as Wolf eating a Whale.

The raising of this pole marked a turning point in pride on the islands, sparking a rebuilding of Haida culture and nationhood that continues still.

81 LOCATION: *Old Masset*
CARVER: *Reg Davidson with Richard Baker*
CULTURAL STYLE: *Haida*

At the north end of Old Masset, east of the grassy sports field, stands the first pole on the Queen Charlotte Islands—in perhaps a century—to be raised for a house and its chief. The name of the house is K'a·adsnee, meaning Shark House. Claude Davidson acquired the name from an uncle through whom he traces his lineage and who had a traditional house by that name at Howkwan in Alaska.

The front door, carved with the Bear Mother story, opens into Claude and Sarah Davidson's gift shop. Behind is their home. The totem pole in front of their house was raised during a potlatch and celebration on 21 and 22 November 1986. The first day saw a solemn ceremony in memory of Claude's brother, Alfred, and his wife, Rose, with the pole being raised the following day.

The log for the pole came from Port Clements. Claude's son, Reg, had assisted in carving many poles before, but this was the first on his own, and he found it a tremendous amount of work. "Towards the end we were working from daybreak to sundown, twelve hours at a stretch," he said. Glen Rabina joined the carvers near the end, and they met the deadline.

"Raising the pole was really difficult and dangerous," Reg said. "Because gale force winds were blowing against the direction of its raising, we had to use four pulling ropes" (instead of the customary two).

That evening, at a large feast and potlatch, Claude Davidson was made the hereditary chief of Dadens, a historic and long-abandoned village on Langara Island, off the northwest tip of the Queen Charlotte Islands.

Dominating the top of the pole is Shark, holding Whale in its teeth. Supporting Shark is Raven, and at his feet is a woman who represents Sarah Davidson. She wears a labret to signify high rank, and on her spruce root hat is painted an Eagle (on the left) with a round eye, and Raven (on the right) with an ovoid-shaped eye.

At the base of the pole stands Grizzly Bear, the main crest of the owner of the pole, together with Frog, a crest given to Sarah. As a non-native, she was officially adopted into the lineage on the day of her marriage to Claude, on 19 December 1975.

147

82/83/84 LOCATION: *Ninstints, Anthony Island*
CARVER: *Not known*
CULTURAL STYLE: *Haida*

6 ft.
1.8 m

The decaying poles that still stand—or sometimes lie—in the long-abandoned villages on the Queen Charlotte Islands give a haunting glimpse of their former power and grandeur. Most notable of the early village sites is Ninstints on Anthony Island (Skungwai to the Haida people), where some sixteen poles line the crescent beachfront of this small offshore island, abandoned by 1880.

In 1957 many of the largest and best-preserved poles were taken down and sent to major museums in Victoria and Vancouver to prevent further decay. Yet there still remained sufficient poles and house remains of significance to warrant UNESCO, in 1981, to declare Ninstints "A World Heritage Site, of importance to the history of Mankind."

Practically all the carved monuments left at Ninstints are mortuary poles, all with their frontal boards missing, although one still retains the planks that closed the top of the burial cavity, together with some of the rocks that held down the planks.

Illustrated are three of these poles: their main crests are, from left to right: Eagle (the beak attached separately, has fallen away), Whale (dorsal fin in the centre, upturned tail flukes at the base), and Grizzly Bear.

Ninstints is protected by law and by onsite custodians. A permit is required from the Haida Band Council, Skidegate, British Columbia V0T 1S0, to visit this and other early village sites.

85 LOCATION: *Prince Rupert—Museum of Northern British Columbia, McBride St. and 1st Ave.*

CARVER: *Dempsey Bob with Glen Wood*

CULTURAL STYLE: *Nishga (Tsimshian)*

Standing tall beside the small but interesting Museum of Northern British Columbia (well worth a visit), is a pole named Eagle on Decayed Pole. It is the fourth reincarnation of a pole that belonged to an Eagle family at Gitlakdamix on the Nass River. The original was destroyed by fire, and the second pole (carved in the early 1890s from a photograph) was taken to the Royal British Columbia Museum, where it now stands by the ground floor escalator.

Carved for the third time in the early 1960s by William Jeffrey, the pole eventually blew down in a tremendous windstorm, breaking into several pieces with parts of it shattered. It was hauled to the city works yard where a workman began bucking it up for firewood, but luckily he was stopped in time and the remaining sections went to the city's museum for preservation.

In 1978 well-known carvers Dempsey Bob and Glen Wood were commissioned to replicate the pole once again. "We worked on it right here, beside the museum," said Dempsey. "A lot of people, locals and tourists, came to watch."

The pole, finished with a minimum amount of paint (as was traditional), shows some of the figures associated with the migration of the Eagle people from the north to the Nass River. Two Eagles perch side by side atop the pole above a Gitksan human crest. "The head once had a row of tufts of hair hanging from its forehead," Dempsey explained, "but ten years of wind and weather have worn them to stubby bristles, which you can see." Beneath are two rows of three human figures, followed by Split-Person (notice the head), and then White Marten. Below are two brothers and their uncle who feature in the family history, and at the base is Eagle-Person representing the Eagle family who owned the pole.

6 ft.
1.8 m

86 LOCATION: *Prince Rupert—Museum of Northern British Columbia, McBride St. and 1st Ave.*
CARVER: *Alvin Adkins with Dale Campbell, Terry Campbell*
CULTURAL STYLE: *Haida*

Just east of the Museum of Northern British Columbia, on Market Place, stands a simple wooden shed that would hardly be noticed—if it were not for the fine pole fronting the gabled building. The structure is a carvers' shed, a workshop facility for northern native carvers who pay an annual fee to make use of it. During the summer the doors often will be open, affording a chance for visitors to watch artists working on a small argillite sculpture, making silver jewellery, carving a mask, a bowl or perhaps even a totem pole.

Haida artist Alvin Adkins designed the carving shed's frontal pole, while the brother and sister team of Tahltan/Tlingit carvers, Dale and Terry Campbell, assisted in the carving. Sponsored by the nearby museum, the pole also provided an opportunity for less experienced carvers to learn as they worked on the cedar log with adze and chisel.

Eagle tops this pole, which has the classic Haida Beaver at its base. Between is the often depicted Nanasimget story of the man whose wife was abducted by a Whale. She is shown upside-down, clinging to Whale's body, with the dorsal fin protruding above her hands. The centre of the pole carries Whale's head, with the blowhole shown as a circle on its forehead. The pole was raised with due ceremony in 1981.

87 LOCATION: *Prince Rupert—Moose Tot Park, 6th Ave. and McBride St.*
CARVER: *Freda Diesing with Josiah Tait*
CULTURAL STYLE: *Haida*

An excellent replica of an old, classic Haida pole towers above the children who frequent the playground where it stands.

The original was a house pole on the southernmost dwelling in a long row of houses at Tanu, a large, once thriving village on the Queen Charlotte Islands. In 1939, when the abandoned village was heavily overgrown with vegetation, the pole was cut down and taken to Prince Rupert for display. Seventeen more years of weathering took their toll, and in 1965 the pole was taken to Victoria to be housed inside the Royal British Columbia Museum.

Freda Diesing, a Haida carver, was commissioned to carve a replica. She had studied at the Gitanmaax School of Northwest Coast Indian Art in 'Ksan, and became only the second woman, after Ellen Neel, to carve totem poles. She worked on the pole with Josiah Tait (father of carver Norman Tait), and together they finished the pole in 1974.

As is typical of many Haida poles, this one is topped by three Watchmen. Below is Eagle holding a staff and with a human face on its upturned tail. Beneath is probably Owl (possibly Hawk), with a short downturned beak, holding an object in its humanlike hands. Next is an abbreviated Whale, depicted only by its round snouted head and upturned tail flukes, followed by Grizzly Bear and Frog. In the Haida tradition, only red and black have been used sparingly in painting the pole.

151

6 ft.
1.8 m

88 LOCATION: *Kitsumkalum—4 km (2½ miles) west of Terrace on Highway 16*
CARVER: *Freda Diesing with a team of assistants*
CULTURAL STYLE: *Northern*

On the north side of the highway, close to a native Indian gift shop (worth a visit), stand two tall totem poles—the first to be raised in the village in more than 150 years. Both were carved by a team mainly of women: Freda Diesing, Dorothy Horner, Myrtle Laidlaw and Sandra Westly, with the help of two young men, Norman Horner (Dorothy's son) and Norman Guno.

The Kitsumkalum Band commissioned the first pole, illustrated here, which incorporates the crests of all the families in the village. The pole is topped by Robin (the band's name means "people of the robin"), below which is a man holding a fish. He represents We-gyet (or Big Man), the supernatural human/ raven of Gitksan lore who brought salmon to all the rivers. Below, in descending order, are Frog, Wolf, Raven, Killer Whale and Eagle. At the base, three figures represent the Bear Mother story: Bear, with a cub between its ears, holds his human wife in front of him. Each carver completed a crest figure, with Freda Diesing supervising.

In a unique ceremony on 1 August 1987, both poles were raised at a major celebration called Su-sit-'aatk, which means "a new beginning." The event, which also included the installation of a high-ranking chief, expressed the intention of the villagers to revitalize their culture.

A unique event at Kitsumkalum—the simultaneous raising of two totem poles, 1987.
PHOTOGRAPH BY JAMES MCDONALD

89 LOCATION: *Kitsumkalum—4 km (2½ miles) west of Terrace on Highway 16*
CARVER: *Freda Diesing with a team of assistants*
CULTURAL STYLE: *Tsimshian, Upper Skeena River*

The second and shorter of the two Kitsumkalum poles is largely a replica of an old pole that once stood in the village but which was swept away during a major flood more than a hundred years ago. This replacement pole was carved from an early photograph by the same team that created the first Kitsumkalum pole, plus a fifth woman, Lorraine McCarthy, not long after they finished their first pole. "The formal style," Freda Diesing said, "is that of the Upper Skeena River area a century ago, depicting humans and animals rather than birds, and with very little paint."

The entire carving represents the Bear Mother story, as did the original, but with the addition of the Kitsumkalum Robin perched on top of a tall hat worn by one of the brothers searching for the abducted woman. Beneath is Bear, and in the centre of the pole is a cavity that represents the cave in which the Bear family lived in hiding. The animals flanking the cavity are the dogs of the hunters searching for them. Below is the Bear Mother holding one of her cubs, with her Bear husband at the base.

In replicating the old pole, the carvers preferred to use the full length of the log rather than cut it, so the hunter's hat was elongated and the village crest added to the top.

To emphasize the links between the past and the present, the band raised the two poles using both old and new methods. The recarved pole was raised by hand-hauled ropes in the traditional manner, while the ropes of the modern pole ran through pulleys to ease the task. Elder Victor Reece directed the difficult operations for both. An estimated two thousand people gathered for the elaborate ceremony and feast that followed. It was an outstanding occasion.

Sitting near the Kitsumkalum poles, I talked with one of the carvers, Dorothy Horner, who recounted the hard work involved in adzing and carving, day after day, for weeks and months on end. Then she added, "It felt good, it made you feel calm. I miss it now—I'd like to do another."

6 ft.
1.8 m

90 LOCATION: *Terrace—RCMP Headquarters, 3205 Eby St.*
CARVER: *Freda Diesing with Dorothy Horner, Vernon Horner, Norman Guno*
CULTURAL STYLE: *Northern*

As a longtime resident of Terrace, carver and artist Freda Diesing felt that it would help to foster good relations between the citizens of Terrace and the people of Kitsumkalum if the native people donated a totem pole to the city to commemorate its diamond jubilee.

Three carvers from the team that made the Kitsumkalum poles carved their own crests from Diesing's design. Vernon Horner worked on his Robin crest at the top, which also represented the band; his mother, Dorothy Horner, carved Eagle in the centre, and Norman Guno carved Whale at the base. Whale's head, with its large teeth and circular blowhole, is uppermost, with a flipper at each side, a protruding dorsal fin on the back and symmetrical tail flukes at the base.

On 29 July 1987, the mayor, Royal Canadian Mounted Police, civic dignitaries and townspeople joined with the people of Kitsumkalum to witness the ceremony in which Chief Clifford Bolton officially presented the pole to the city of Terrace. In a speech, he explained that the crests represented progress and future development, as well as being the crests of "the carvers and the people of Kitsumkalum—which people shall be forever present."

154

BACKGROUND TO 'KSAN
NEAR HAZELTON

The replica Gitksan village of 'Ksan, on the Skeena River, near Hazelton, 1977. PHOTOGRAPH BY HILARY STEWART

On the banks of the Upper Skeena River, near Hazelton in north central British Columbia, amid spectacular scenery, stands the village of 'Ksan. Its single row of traditional plank houses with painted fronts and a cluster of totem poles stand where Indian villages have stood for thousands of years.

'Ksan originated in the early 1950s as an attempt to solve the social and economic problems of Hazelton (population then 432) and to promote understanding and respect for the native people and their traditions. It began with a single building to house and display the ceremonial artifacts and regalia of many chiefs, who had access to them when needed. Quality native crafts were also available for visitors to purchase. Over the years, the success of this small museum, called The Treasure House, eventually led to the idea of building an entire village as it would have been a hundred years ago.

Through the co-operation of local, provincial and federal governments, the necessary funding was raised, and 'Ksan was officially opened on 12 August 1970 with great ceremony and jubilation.

'Ksan is a reconstructed Gitksan village, with traditional style buildings that house a museum, an exhibit hall, the only existing school for Northwest Coast Indian art, a gift shop selling authentic local native work and a feast house where visitors can witness traditional native dances and ceremonies. A large campsite beside the river caters to visitors from around the world. There is no entry fee to the village.

The name 'Ksan means "river of mists," though anglicization has changed the river's name to Skeena. The prefix *git* means "people of," thus the Gitksan of the Hazelton area are the people of the river of mists. The revival of their performing arts includes a large, well-costumed dance group, which has performed internationally. They have termed 'Ksan "the Breath of our Grandfathers." Inspired by the past, born in the present and bequeathed to the future, the arts of 'Ksan continue to enjoy success and popularity. Understanding and respect for their traditions have indeed become a reality.

155

6 ft.
1.8 m

91 LOCATION: *'Ksan—at the entrance*
CARVER: *Carvers of 'Ksan*
CULTURAL STYLE: *'Ksan (Tsimshian)*

Although an archway to mark an entrance is not a traditional concept in Northwest Coast Indian culture, nevertheless the twin crest poles joined by carved and painted planks form an inviting entrance to the renowned replica village of 'Ksan.

Each pole carries figures of people and creatures found in Gitksan histories and traditions. Some of the legendary tales, extremely long and complex, were told by expert speakers who excelled in the art of storytelling.

At the top is Eagle, and beneath him crouches a small Frog, whose hind legs appear in the ears of the figure below. Many legends of the Upper Skeena River people contain elaborate episodes pertaining to frogs, and there is a variety of crests that are derived from these.

The creature below Frog is the mythical Hawk, a supernatural bird having a sharply recurved beak as well as a mouth with teeth. The next figure is that of a chief holding a staff, and below him is Beaver with large incisor teeth, holding a chewing stick, and with the customary cross-hatched tail having a face at the joint. The poles are painted red and black.

The two cedar planks that form the arch are similar to those once used in house construction. Boards of great width and length were split from cedar logs to build the walls and roof of a house, as well as the interior platforms.

To pass through the arched entrance and to walk along the pathway into the village of 'Ksan is to take a journey back in time.

92 LOCATION: *'Ksan*

CARVER: *Duane Pasco and 'Ksan carvers*

CULTURAL STYLE: *'Ksan (Tsimshian)*

The opening of the village of 'Ksan on 12 August 1970 called for great ceremony, and a special totem pole was raised to commemorate the jubilant event. Called The Meeting Place, the pole carries figures representing the three local clans.

Standing stiffly to attention on the top of the pole, and looking somewhat out of place, is a white man—a British Columbia government representative, complete with top hat and bow tie. At his feet are leaves of the dogwood tree, its flower being the official floral emblem of the province. In native culture the "top man on the totem pole" does not infer superiority; in fact, the opposite holds true. It is the large figure at the base that is the strongest and most powerful.

Beneath the white man is Eagle, representing a small clan of the area, and below is a crouched Wolf, with a long snout and upright ears, representing the Wolf clan. At the base is a crest of the dominant Fireweed clan—Mosquito transforming into a human, with wings giving way to arms and the human legs already in place. A small Frog is visible on Mosquito's forehead—a part of the story that goes with the crest.

6 ft.
1.8 m

157

93 LOCATION: *'Ksan*
CARVER: *Duane Pasco with local carvers*
CULTURAL STYLE: *'Ksan (Tsimshian)*

Because 'Ksan is a simulated village, the poles created for it do not carry valid cultural significance, except for the opening day ceremonial pole. Thus, the lofty monuments, though carved in the traditional art form, are also simulated. Family crests and story figures shown are somewhat hybrid versions of the real thing.

This pole, for instance, loosely portrays the Bear Mother story. It is topped by one of the brothers, and below is Bear, with the woman he abducted shown peeking out over his thighs. The next two figures portray the Bear Mother and her Bear husband, but the design includes three cubs instead of the traditional two. A small Frog fills the space below Bear's paws.

This was the first pole raised in the 'Ksan project. Sheltered by a lean-to shed, the carvers began working on it in October 1969 and continued on into the cold weather of the north. By the time the pole was ready for painting, the plunging temperature and cold winds turned the paint into a jellylike paste, making continuous painting impossible. To overcome the problem, the carvers worked in relays. Duane said, "One man would heat his can of paint indoors, then run out and apply the paint for as long as it stayed liquid; then another man would replace him with a warmed can of paint and continue the work." Eventually, in spite of freezing cold fingers, even in gloves, the job was finished.

94 LOCATION: *Hazelton—at the foot of Government St.*
CARVER: *Not known*
CULTURAL STYLE: *Gitksan (Tsimshian)*

Carved around 1889, this pole was at one time the tallest in the Indian reserve at Gitenmaaks—now Hazelton. It was relocated and now stands on the banks of the Skeena River, beside an old paddle wheel, next to the local museum.

The upper third of the pole, adzed into a square shaft, may have been topped by a crest figure in early times. The uppermost figure is Corpse Split in Two, and beneath is Nose Like Coho, two crests whose origin and significance have been lost to antiquity. The delicately carved Frogs on the forehead of Nose Like Coho represent the Flying Frogs crest.

Below is probably the spirit name of the chief of the family that owned the pole: Man of the Wilds (or Bush Man). He is gently holding a small frog in his cupped hands in the same manner that a shaman holds a patient's soul.

Next is a row of three children, which depicts a dramatic spirit device enacted in the winter ceremonials: unclad children of the household lay in one direction on the floor in the centre of the house (which symbolized the river), to represent the salmon running upstream. The figure at the base is either a crest figure called Halfway Out (of the door), or Man of the Wilds again.

This pole is especially noteworthy for its interesting details, which can easily be missed: note the two different facial expressions on the two halves of Corpse Split in Two, as well as one palm turned in, the other out. Also, look for the small oval faces (sideways on) carved into Nose Like Coho's knees and elbows—the one on the right knee is the best preserved. In addition, note the hooked nose that gives Nose Like Coho his name.

159

6 ft.
1.8 m

95/96 LOCATION: *Kispiox—Kispiox Band Office*
CARVER: *Walter Harris*
CULTURAL STYLE: *Gitksan (Tsimshian)*

An attractive band office and cultural centre building stands beside the road at the entrance to the old village of Kispiox, which is well known for its totem poles.

A red-and-black painted split-design of Raven stealing the Sun fills the triangle formed by the building's roof gable, while Eagle and Raven decorate the double front doors. In addition, two fine unpainted poles flank the entrance and proclaim the identity of the band.

Part of the colourful ceremony that officially opened the new building in October 1978 was the ceremonial carrying of the two totem poles from the nearby carving site to the entrance of the building, and the subsequent raising of them. Speech-making, drumming and singing by elders in ceremonial regalia culminated in a speech, in his native tongue, by eighty-five-year-old Moses Morrison. As he cut the ribbon, he called out in English, "We are all united!"

The pole on the left has Bear with a salmon at the top. In the centre is Raven, and at the base is the figure of the legendary Ya-l, the founder of the Kispiox people, holding a weapon. In ancient times there was but one village, Temlaham, where lived a wicked man named Ya-l. He would kill at the slightest provocation, then flee to a hiding place, but he always returned with many beaver skins. One day a boy taunted the snow, causing a local winter, and the people left the village. One group, led by Ya-l, moved to his hide-out, which he had named Kispiox, meaning "place of hiding."

The pole on the right depicts Frog at the top. Below is long-snouted Wolf holding his long tail, followed by a classic Beaver with its cross-hatched, up-turned tail, round nostrils and two large incisor teeth.

The well-known artist and carver Walter Harris, who lives in Kispiox, worked on the poles alone.

Leaning totem poles in Kispiox, prior to the 1920s restoration project; some of these are still standing. COURTESY ROYAL BRITISH COLUMBIA MUSEUM, NO. 7960

6 ft.
1.8 m

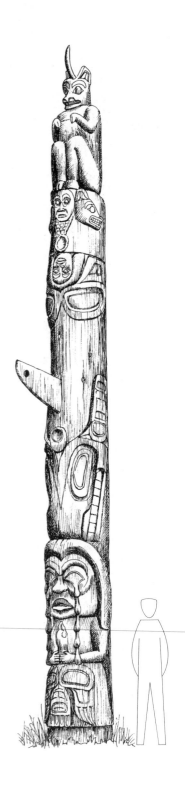

97 LOCATION: *Kispiox*
CARVER: *Walter Harris, Earl Muldoe, Vic Mowatt*
CULTURAL STYLE: *Gitksan (Tsimshian)*

Raised in 1973 with all due ceremony, this fine pole carries ancient and interesting stories.

At the top is a family crest—the One-Horned Mountain Goat. It is said that in the ancient past, at the village of Temlaham, the people no longer regarded animals with respect. Recklessly, they slaughtered herds of mountain goats on the mountain now called Rocher Deboule, near Hazelton. They took one young goat home as a trophy, but a youth of the village took it for a pet, rescuing it from abuse.

In revenge, the remainder of the goats, in human form, invited the offenders to a feast at their mountain lodge. Unaccustomed to such craggy terrain, the villagers fell to their deaths in the night—all except the youth who had been kind to the young goat. In gratitude, the sure-footed animal led him down the peaks to safety, and thus his family adopted as a crest the goat with a single horn on its head.

Beneath One-Horned Mountain Goat are Wolf heads flanking a humanlike head. Around the being's mask, a complete abalone shell and sections of shell are inlaid; they reflect the sunshine on a bright day. A somewhat obscure story, clouded in uncertainty, relates to a supernatural being who wore a magnificent necklace, part of which was a figure representing the Sun.

The central figure on the pole, White Whale, is shown head downward, complete with blowhole, dorsal fin and other whale attributes.

The beautifully carved Weeping Woman at the base tells of a time when there was starvation in the land. Two sisters and their brother set out in search of food; but having no luck, they grew weak, and eventually the brother succumbed. No sooner had he died than the sisters saw a grouse, which they captured, cooked and ate; but it had come just too late to save their brother. The carved figure shows a grieving sister holding a grouse to her, with its body, tail and wings carved to create a design on her skirt.

98 LOCATION: *Kispiox*
CARVER: *Walter Harris*
CULTURAL STYLE: *Gitksan (Tsimshian)*

The original of this pole was carved sometime in the first decade of the twentieth century to commemorate a member of the Qael family, belonging to the Fireweed phratry (one of three main crest divisions that include Frog and Wolf). Tradition required that the carving of a pole be done by a person of another phratry. Because the carver of this pole was within the same phratry, a man of a different phratry was appointed in charge of the work as nominal carver, to "stand over" the work.

Walter Harris, an experienced and skilled carver of Kispiox, and a member of the house of Qael, repeated history when he replicated the old pole. He appointed his uncle, Jeffrey Harris, who was from a different phratry, to "stand over" the work, or "to take the credit for carving the pole," as he put it.

The new pole is a precise copy of the early carving. The top figure, an ancient crest called Leading In, is a being with a humanlike face and a very large mouth. Beneath is another crest figure called Glass Nose (also Ice Nose or Sharp Nose), the name being descriptive of its facial feature. The long, carved nose has now fallen away, revealing the slot in the pole into which it was fitted. The small head on the chest may represent Grizzly Bear Woman, another crest of the Qael family. Leading In is represented twice more on the lower half of the pole.

This cedar document was raised in 1972, a major event that brought high-ranking chiefs and guests from far and wide to witness and celebrate with traditional ceremonies and feasting.

6 ft.
1.8 m

163

99 LOCATION: *Kispiox*
CARVER: *Earl Muldoe*
CULTURAL STYLE: *Gitksan (Tsimshian)*

Erected in 1845 as a memorial to a chief named Gitludahl, the White Owl pole was at one time among the oldest in Kispiox. Some forty years later, a pole named Grizzly Bear of the Sun was raised for another chief of the same name. Both poles are now gone.

The pole that now stands in Kispiox was carved in 1973 and belongs to Pete Muldoe; it combines the crests from both these old poles.

At the top is White Owl, with a small figure carved in each ear, another standing on its forehead and a row of three humans below. Beneath is Grizzly Bear of the Sun. The origin of this crest is said to go back to when Kispiox was first established, when ancestors of the pole's owner were at their fish camp at Salmon Creek, opposite present-day Kispiox. A young girl, secluded in a small hut as part of her puberty rites, saw a bear coming down the creek with a "sun collar" around its neck. Her parents killed the animal and gave her the emblem to use as a crest for her offspring.

Below Grizzly Bear of the Sun is a repeat of White Owl, then three human figures, two of which have headgear representing tendrils of the Fern crest. Notice that the pole was carved (as was the original) on an inverted log, so that the wide base of the tree was uppermost.

100 LOCATION: *Kispiox*
CARVER: *Salomon Johnson*
CULTURAL STYLE: *Gitksan (Tsimshian)*

This very old pole, thought to have been erected in the 1860s, is part of the family history of Alice Wilson who lives in Kispiox. It was originally raised, she said, by Simon Williams, a chief whose native name was Ha·waw. At his death, that name was passed on to her uncle, Simon Williams, and thence to Alice Wilson herself, who now proudly carries the name Chief Ha·waw.

The pole was originally topped by a horizontal Wolf, a family emblem known as Raiding Wolf, and of which the owner had a mask. Beneath the uncarved section, Wolf is depicted again, head down, but with its ears (which were separate attachments) now lost; notice the slots into which they were affixed.

The next figure is a crest named Running Backwards, as is the bottom figure. The haunches and legs of the base figure are turned backwards (as can be seen in an early photo of the pole), but over time they have become buried—possibly as a result of restoring the leaning pole to an upright position in the 1920s.

Between these two figures is depicted a family emblem named Hole Through, which represents a house front device. Above the regular door of the house was a circular doorway, with several small humanlike beings around it, their feet facing the rim. This served as a ceremonial entrance to the house whenever a feast was given. Then, the door below was blocked, and ladders inside and out gave access to the house through the hole. Although badly weathered now, the small figures with their delicately detailed fingers and thumbs are a fine example of the woodcarver's skill.

Detail of the Hole Through pole, showing finely carved figures. PHOTOGRAPH BY HILARY STEWART

6 ft.
1.8 m

165

6 ft.
1.8 m

101 LOCATION: *Ketchikan, Alaska—Tongass Historical Society Museum*
CARVER: *Dempsey Bob*
CULTURAL STYLE: *Tlingit*

The story of Raven stealing the Sun and bringing daylight to the world is often depicted by that bird carrying a disc in his beak. Here, all the characters in the story are brought together to create an entire pole.

At the top of the pole is the culture hero, Raven, with a six-rayed Sun beneath him. Below is the chief's daughter, who wears a labret to signify her high rank; at the base is the chief himself, wearing a tall hat to indicate his wealth and rank. The small face of the baby, encircled in black to suggest his raven-ness, has been carved into the chief's hat.

This pole, named Raven Stealing the Sun, was raised on 21 May 1983, and honours the Tongass Tlingit people.

The Fog Woman pole, as it is called, was carved in 1981 by the well-known Tlingit carver Nathan Jackson as a memorial to the Tongass people of the area. It illustrates the ancient story of how the first salmon came to the rivers.

Raven and his two slaves were fishing, but caught only bullheads. When fog came up, they began paddling back to their fish camp; suddenly, a young woman appeared in their canoe. She was Fog Woman, the daughter of Chief Fog on the Salmon, and Raven took her for his wife.

Skilled at basketry, Fog Woman made a finely woven, watertight basket of spruce root, and Raven complimented her on it. "Watch what it can do," she said; as she dipped her hands into the fresh water in the basket, a large salmon appeared. Daily, Fog Woman dipped her hands in the basket; and daily, a salmon appeared. Soon the fish-drying rack was hung with rows and rows of dried and smoked salmon, and the storehouse was filled to capacity.

Raven's boasting of his success in acquiring so much salmon angered his wife, and they quarrelled fiercely. Eventually, Raven hit Fog Woman with a dried salmon, and she ran out of the house and down to the beach, her husband following. She went into the sea, and as Raven reached out to grab her, she turned into fog. Then all the dried and smoked salmon left the storehouse and the racks and followed her into the sea, leaving Raven holding only a bullhead.

Nathan Jackson's pole is topped by Raven holding a lumpy, inedible bullhead; beneath are portrayed the two slaves, also with bullheads on their lines. Below is Fog Woman with a salmon in one hand and in the other a representation of a copper, symbol of her wealth, while at her feet are the first salmon she brought forth out of her basket of fresh water. Nowadays, Fog Woman's daughter, Creek Woman, lives at the head of every stream, and it is she who brings the salmon back up the streams every year.

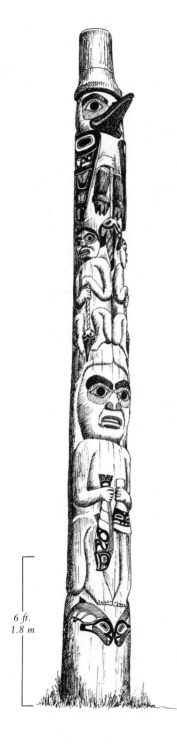

6 ft.
1.8 m

167

A section of Totem Bight State Park, showing the traditional Tlingit style house, portal pole, carved corner post and crest pole, 1976. PHOTOGRAPH BY HILARY STEWART

BACKGROUND TO TOTEM BIGHT STATE PARK
NEAR KETCHIKAN, ALASKA

In an attractive waterfront setting, Totem Bight State Park brings together a large collection of northern totem poles and a traditional plank house.

In the 1930s, when the United States Forest Service realized that many fine poles were falling into decay, it began an ambitious program to create a replica Tlingit village. The site chosen was Mud Bight in Tongass National Forest, 16 km (10 miles) north of Ketchikan. Appropriately, the sheltered cove with a wide gravel bar and salmon creek had once been a Tlingit campsite for many generations. Much of the work was done by the Civilian Conservation Corps, an organization set up by the U.S. government to provide employment during the 1930s Depression.

The project called for dwellings, smoke houses and gravehouses, together with totem and mortuary poles from the various Tlingit groups, as well as from the Haida. The poles would be replicas of old poles from deserted villages and new ones carved especially for the site.

Work began in 1938, with head carver Charles Brown supervising workers in the construction of a plank house with a portal pole, carved corner posts, a memorial pole in front and another out on the point.

Unfortunately, the United States' entry into the Second World War prevented completion of the project. However, additional carved poles representative of the Tlingit and Haida have been added over the years; the uninviting name of Mud Bight was changed to Totem Bight, and the park now displays an impressive collection of totem poles. A plaque on the back of each gives some brief information about the carvings.

LOCATION: *Ketchikan, Alaska—Totem Bight State Park*
CARVER: *John Wallace*
CULTURAL STYLE: *Haida*

North of the community house is the Master Carpenter pole, one of the few remaining poles originally carved for Totem Bight State Park. It was created in 1947 by John Wallace, a Haida from Hydaburg, Alaska, who was former head of the Civilian Conservation Corps carving project.

John Wallace carved the pole to depict several crests belonging to the Eagle and Raven clans of the Haida people. Beneath Eagle, who tops the pole, is Beaver holding his chewing stick, followed by Bullhead. Next is Raven, then Bear—notice the two very small coppers under his feet and Frog between. Next is Blackfish, or Killer Whale, represented by its head and pectoral fins only, followed by Master Carpenter, with Owl at the base.

Legend tells that it was Master Carpenter who taught the Haida to carve. He appeared to them wearing a richly ornamented garment of mountain goat wool and a carved and painted headdress. Tattoo crests adorned his body, and on his fingernails were human faces, each with a different expression, while a bright light shone around him. He bade the people to go to bed as usual, to pay no attention to what they might hear, and to not look until the sun was up. In the night they heard chopping sounds but refrained from looking until the sun rose; then they saw that the house poles had been carved and that the partition at the rear of the house had been painted all over with human and animal figures in wondrous designs. Outside, they saw carved poles and posts, and the front of the house was all carved and painted. Master Carpenter came daily, instructing the men in the skills of design, carving and painting, as well as in the spiritual training required for successful work.

On this pole the figure of Master Carpenter is painted in a light colour to represent the halo around him. His garments are embellished and he has a tattoo on his face. Even his eyes carry designs. Since the fingernails were too small to show the faces, Wallace carved them in the form of a necklace. Down each side of the carpenter figure, he added a fish club ornamented with a Shark (or Dogfish) and a Bear, both Raven clan crests.

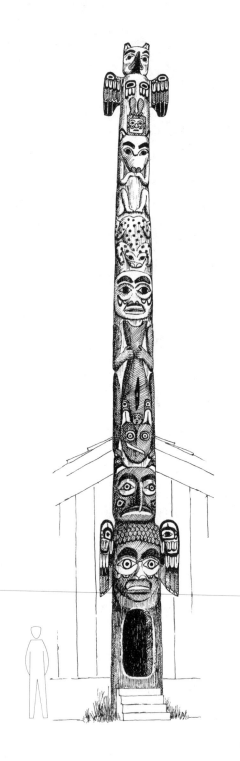

104 LOCATION: *Ketchikan, Alaska—Totem Bight State Park*
CARVER: *Charles Brown*
CULTURAL STYLE: *Tlingit*

The large plank house with its painted front and carved house posts is a feature of the park; though it is modelled after a nineteenth-century house, such decorated dwellings were not common. Inside, the two carved house posts that support the large cedar beams depict the story of Duk-tooth, a man who proved his strength by tearing a sea lion in two.

Outside the house is the portal pole called Wandering Raven, which carries figures that illustrate several legends. Raven, the legendary light-bringer, stands at the top of the pole, his feet on the box containing the Sun. Beneath Raven is Mink, a powerful spirit helper of a well-known shaman who not only cured the sick but could foresee events.

The next figure is Frog, recalling a lengthy story of a young woman who met and married a man who, though he appeared human, was really a Frog. The man took her to his father's house in his village. One day the woman's relatives saw her sitting on a marshy spot in the middle of the lake, along with a large Frog and a young one, then they disappeared. The relatives drained the lake and recovered the young woman, who told them of her experiences.

Below Frog is a man named Natsihlane holding Whale. A long and involved story ends with Natsihlane planning to kill his brothers-in-law, who had tried to kill him. He carved a wooden whale, then built a chain of four pools on the beach, the last leading into the sea. When he put the carving of the whale into the first pool, it made a leap, then sank. He tried carving whales of various woods; some made it to the second or the third pool, but none came fully alive. Finally, he carved a whale of yellow cedar, and it swam through the pools to the sea. Natsihlane told it to find the canoe of his brothers-in-law and destroy it so that they would drown. When this was accomplished, Natsihlane instructed the Whale to never again harm human beings. And it never has.

Beneath Whale is Raven at the Head of the Nass, the chief who owned the Sun, identified by his recurved beak, feathered breast and wings; below him is his wife, who wears a large labret.

BACKGROUND TO KIKS'ADI TOTEM PARK
WRANGELL, ALASKA

COURTESY ALASKA DIVISION OF TOURISM

The shore of Wrangell harbour was once the site of many totem poles. As the town grew, facilities for fishboats and an active marine community eventually displaced many of them. The poles were in varying stages of decay, and the toppling of a fine old one, the Raven pole, in a windstorm in 1978, proved to be the motivation for a major restoration project. Many other old poles were taken down for preservation and replication.

In 1984 a native group named the Wrangell Cultural Heritage Committee commissioned the replication of four of the early poles. On behalf of the committee, the Sealaska Corporation purchased the Front St. waterfront site on which one early pole still stood, and this became Kiks'adi Totem Park, dedicated on 2 July 1987 with all due ceremony.

The two carvers who undertook the task of recarving the decayed poles were Steve Brown, an experienced non-native carver from Seattle, Washington, with many years of Northwest Coast Indian studies and practice behind him, and Wayne Price, a talented young Tlingit carver from Haines, Alaska. Since Steve was right-handed and Wayne left-handed, they made an efficient team, each working on opposite sides of a pole. They worked in a specially constructed shed in downtown Wrangell, with the original pole lying close to the new log. To further ensure precise replication, they studied early photographs, took measurements and made templates of the originals.

Steve Brown said, "Wayne and I had such admiration and respect for those old works that we tried very hard and took great pains to make them as true as we possibly could. We tried to leave 'ourselves' out of the variables." The results carry the visitor back a hundred years or more.

6 ft.
1.8 m

105 LOCATION: *Wrangell, Alaska—Kiks'adi Totem Park*
CARVER: *Steve Brown and Wayne Price*
CULTURAL STYLE: *Tlingit*

Known as the Kiks'adi pole, this "centrepiece" pole standing on the site of the original gives the park its name. The original, carved about 1890 by William Ukas, was raised to honour a Kiks'adi clan chief named Kohlteen. The monument is also known as the Kohlteen pole.

Carver Steve Brown told me about an interesting aspect of this work. "When it came time to carve the pole," he said, "some of the grandchildren of the original carver came to us with the request that we do the carving without using any power tools. William Ukas's son, Thomas, was also a carver of totem poles and did not think chainsaws and other power tools appropriate to totem pole art. We were inclined to agree."

The two carvers worked through the winter of 1985–86. "Using only hand tools that we could see had been used by the original artist, such as handsaws, chisels, an auger bit and traditional adzes, we completed the work in five months."

Still holding to tradition, the Kiks'adi pole was raised by hand at the dedication of the park on 2 June 1987. The celebration included dancers and drummers from Juneau and Ketchikan.

The pole is topped by a personified mountain, here shown as Person of the Glacier, to which the Kiks'adi people retreated during the great flood. Below is Frog, the main crest of the Kiks'adi clan of the Stikine Tlingit, followed by Elder Raven "teaching" the younger Raven. At the base is Beaver, with a small Frog emerging from its neck.

The meaning of the small Frog is unclear, but the Beaver crest depicts the well-known Killisnoo. Long ago, a great chief kept a pet Beaver, paying it so much attention that his people felt neglected and were jealous. They taunted and teased the Beaver, named Killisnoo, who became very angry. He went to his pond, transformed into a giant Beaver, and tunnelled under all the houses.

Gnawing on a poplar stick one day, he made a salmon spear and hid it in a hollow tree. Hunters followed the trail of gnawed wood, found the spear, and took it to the chief, who made enquiries as to who had made it. Killisnoo kept insisting, "I made it!" but no one would believe him. To prove that he could handle such a weapon, Killisnoo grabbed the spear and thrust it at the chief, striking him in the heart and killing him. He killed others who tried to prevent his escape, then he slapped his flat tail very hard on the ground; the earth shook, and all the houses collapsed into his underground excavations.

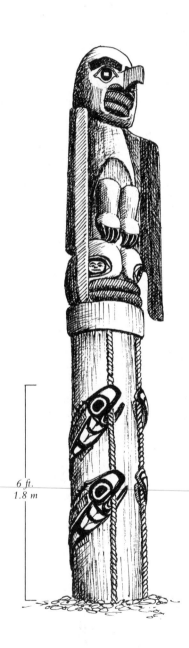

6 ft.
1.8 m

174

Known either as the Kayak pole, or the One-legged Fisherman pole, this replica is one of two poles of similar design. One was raised by Chief Shakes VII, in memory of Kaukish, his sixty-eight-year-old nephew who died in 1897, leaving Shakes all his property. The replica is based on a much earlier pole originally from Old Wrangell village and was made from a photograph taken in 1910 as the original pole did not survive.

The pole represents a lengthy story, owned by Kaukish, about a man named Kayak. It includes an episode about a one-legged fisherman who looked like an Eagle and who wore a coat on which were the heads of two Grizzly Bears. The fisherman owned a magical spear, and this enabled him to take many salmon. With a successful catch on a string, he paddled up the creek until he reached a Grizzly Bear cave. There, one of the heads on his coat pulled a salmon off the string and flung it to a male Grizzly; the other head did the same for a female Grizzly, and so on until all the salmon were given to the Bears.

Kayak coveted the wonderful spear. He put on the skin of a monster and went into the water; when the fisherman threw the spear, Kayak grabbed it. The next day, when the fisherman came looking for his lost spear, Kayak killed him and put on the monster skin together with the coat, then caught a string of salmon. He, too, went up the creek to feed the Bears, but they realized that he was an imposter, and in the ensuing fight Kayak killed the Bear family.

The memorial pole to Kaukish shows the fisherman in Eagle form. The head below is unidentified, but may represent Kayak in the skin of the monster—note the small faces in the eyes and the strings of salmon down the rest of the pole.

107 LOCATION: *Wrangell, Alaska—Kiks'adi Totem Park*
CARVER: *Steve Brown and Wayne Price*
CULTURAL STYLE: *Tlingit*

The original of this memorial pole, carved by William Ukas and raised in 1896, stood at the south end of Church St., on the site of the present Bible Baptist Church.

Dr. Thwing, a missionary in Wrangell at the time, wrote in an item for the local newspaper, *The Alaskan*: "This winter there has been a very special feeling of suspense and expectancy in view of the great feast and intertribal dance for which Chief Shakes has been preparing for a year or two. To dignify a living son, and commemorate one dead, there has been a new totem pole carved, and the Tongass natives have been called to dance and feast here. These guests arrived Feb. 1st, and were received with great honor and noise."

The original pole stood for eighty-two years. Its deeply indented carving allowed rot to hollow much of the centre, and in 1978 a windstorm sent the pole crashing, breaking it into pieces.

The replica pole illustrated here depicts the much-told story of Raven bringing daylight to the world. At the top is Raven at the Head of the Nass, the original keeper of the Sun, shown in both Raven and human form. He sits on the box that contains the Sun. The box is painted to portray an inlay of operculum (a lidlike part of a marine snail shell) around the lid and the base. Below is another Raven with a Sun halo around his head, while on his chest is a female wearing a labret to indicate high rank—perhaps the daughter of the chief who owned the Sun. The Raven below, in another interpretation, is also described as the daughter to whom Raven was born. The figure at the base, wearing a large labret, has also been given variable identities: Tribal Astronomer who led the people during clan migrations, or Woman Who Holds Up the Earth (Raven's mother in an earlier reincarnation).

In spite of the variations in explanation, there is no disputing why this cedar monument is called the Raven pole.

175

Two well-known mortuary poles stand in front of a traditional plank house completed in 1939 by the Civilian Conservation Corps.

This replica of Chief Shakes's house stands on the same site and is of the same construction and dimensions as the original. All the boards, with hand-adzed surfaces, are held in place without nails. Inside are copies of the oldest Tlingit house posts in existence; the originals, which date from around 1780, are in the Wrangell Museum. These replicas were carved by Brown, Price and Burkhart.

The original of the left-hand pole is called the Double Killer Whale Crest Hat pole. A large and elaborate ceremonial crest hat, carved in wood, was the most prestigious object of a Tlingit clan—a prized family heirloom, as revered as a crown would be in another culture. The hat crest on top of this pole, a Nanya·ayi clan heirloom, is comprised of two Whale heads and dorsal fins, back to back, with a column of three skils in the centre. The identity of the figure wearing the hat has been lost in the past.

The original pole appears in an 1868 photo, but there is no crouched figure beneath the man wearing the crest hat. A photo of the 1880s shows the pole replicated, with the crouched figure. The identity of the small crouched figure has also been lost.

Some sixty years later, the decaying replicated pole was accurately copied by the CCC. In a poor state of preservation by 1984, the upper part of the pole, the hat, was again replicated, with the carvers working from photos of the previous poles. The lower vertical section is still the CCC version; it was well preserved, having been protected from the rain by the horizontal hat.

This type of mortuary pole held the ashes of the deceased in a rectangular niche at the back, covered by a wood panel. The replica has two niches, but the ashes of Chief Shakes VI's mother and father were, of course, only in the original.

176

The second of the two mortuary poles standing in front of Chief Shakes's house is known as the Bear up the Mountain pole. The original appeared to be quite new when it was photographed in 1868, but it was sufficiently rotted by the late 1930s to warrant being recarved by the Civilian Conservation Corps. It, too, decayed over the years and part of it, the Bear figure, was again replicated in 1984 by Brown, Price and Burkhart from the 1868 photo.

This crest originated during a time long ago when there was a great flood in the land. As the people of the Nanya·ayi clan were climbing a mountain to escape the rising waters, a Grizzly Bear and a Mountain Goat went along with them, stopping and moving on when the people did.

Ultimately, the Nanya·ayi killed the Grizzly Bear, took it for a crest, and preserved its hide intact. The hide became a valuable and renowned heirloom, which was displayed at potlatches and other important occasions; many slaves, furs and items of value were given away each time it was shown. Over the years this amounted to a great sum. All the Tlingit spoke of the Nanya·ayi clan who took great pride in their ownership of the Grizzly hide; many songs were composed about it, with words such as "Come here, you Bear, the highest Bear of all Bears." When the hide disintegrated with age, it was replaced by another, and then another—up until the present time. The mask-head of this Bear, with copper ear faces, is now in the Thomas Burke Memorial Washington State Museum in Seattle.

This mortuary pole, which originally held the ashes of Chief Shakes's brother, depicts the great Grizzly Bear, with its footprints climbing up the mountain.

There are six other poles on the island, four copies and two originals, all made during the CCC project of 1938–1940.

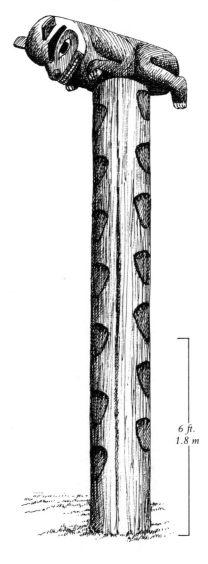

6 ft.
1.8 m

177

110 LOCATION: *Juneau, Alaska—Centennial Hall, Egan Dr.*
CARVER: *Nathan Jackson with Steve Brown*
CULTURAL STYLE: *Tlingit*

Two poles were carved to celebrate Juneau's centennial in 1980, and both stand outside Centennial Hall. This one is called the Wooshkeetaan pole, and it represents the history of the Wooshkeetaan people. George Jim, a respected clan leader from the small but traditional village of Angoon, near Juneau, determined which crests should be on the pole and gave an account of his people's history. The following is a much abbreviated version.

Long ago, a group of Tlingit people migrated along the Taku River, eventually arriving at its mouth. From there, they scattered throughout the southeast of what is now Alaska, with some going to the Wrangell area, some to Klawak and others to Glacier Bay. Eventually the village at Glacier Bay was destroyed by the advancing glacier, and the people from there moved again. Their descendants, the Wooshkeetaan, finally established villages in the Juneau area.

But the late nineteenth century brought other disruptions. With the discovery of gold in Juneau in the 1880s, many native people in surrounding areas were drawn to Juneau and Douglas (across the channel). In 1882 the U.S. Navy, through an unfortunate set of circumstances, bombarded the village of Angoon, looted the partially destroyed village, and smashed canoes. Events such as these, which caused major changes in the life of the people, eventually led to the abandonment of the old villages.

This totem pole carries crests and legends of the Wooshkeetaan people of the Eagle clan. Uncle Sam stands at the top, as a reminder that no apology or compensation has ever been made to the people of Angoon for the navy's actions. Uncle Sam straddles a Shark (or Dogfish), whose dorsal fin is between his knees. Shark's head, flanked by his pectoral fins, has a high dome and gill slits. The bird just beneath Shark's head is Murrelet, a small diving seabird.

The next figure is Eagle, followed by Bear. On Bear's stomach is a crouching Wolf, head down, representing the legend of how a Wolf claimed the Wooshkeetaan as part of his family.

Beneath Wolf is Sea Bear—notice the small fins on his elbows and the upturned tail flukes instead of legs. The next figure is Good Luck Woman who, because she was giving birth in a separate hut behind the village, escaped being killed during a massacre of all the villagers, and who was the source of the regeneration of the clan. She is depicted carrying her infant on her back, behind her left shoulder.

The figure below is Spirit Man, who represents the five powerful Spirit Men of the Wooshkeetaan village in Berner's Bay. The indistinct Halibut on his chest symbolizes his strength. At the base is Berner's Bay Mountain, the ancestral home of all the Wooshkeetaan.

111 LOCATION: *Juneau, Alaska—Centennial Hall, Egan Dr.*
CARVER: *Nathan Jackson with Steve Brown*
CULTURAL STYLE: *Tlingit*

The second of the two poles commissioned for Juneau's centennial, and raised in 1981, is named the Auk Tribe pole. Like the Wooshkeetaan pole, this one speaks of the history of its people—in this case the Raven of the Dipper House. Bessie Vesaya, an elder of the Auk people, advised on what crest figures should be on the pole.

The pole is topped by Raven, who perches on four skils. Below is Monster Frog, crowned by seven stars that represent the celestial Dipper for which the house is named. Legend has it that the chief awoke one night and discovered a monsterlike frog sitting on the roof of his house, declaring that he was the Dipper from the Sky and that should be the name of the house. The human hands on Monster Frog represent his supernaturalness.

Below are two Auk crests. One is Dog Salmon, head downward, its tail and fins attached to the log separately; dash lines represent the spawning colours of the skin, and red is for the eggs. The other crest is Summer Weasel, head down, identified by its long, black-tipped tail.

At the base stands Good Luck Woman and her child (on her left shoulder), also depicted on the Wooshkeetaan pole. When she left the massacred village with her baby, the woman walked along the beach towards what is now Juneau, eating mussels as she went, discarding the shells. It is said that she always ate seven at a time; thus, to find a pathway of mussel shells, or seven of them nested together, is to have good fortune. At the bottom of the pole are carved the seven mussel shells.

Working outdoors in the fall, carvers Nathan Jackson and Steve Brown laboured long and tiring days in a race against the oncoming winter. "We were spurred on," Steve said, "by the sight of the snowline descending ever lower down the steep slopes of Mount Juneau." They made it in time.

112 LOCATION: *Juneau, Alaska—Auk Tribe Building, Village St. and Willoughby Ave.*
CARVER: *Edward Kunz, William Smith, Tom Jimmy, Edward Kunz Jr.*
CULTURAL STYLE: *Tlingit*

Two poles stand in front of a panel on the Auk Tribe Building, which is painted with Tlingit motifs. Both poles were carved in 1972: one honours the Raven clan, and the other the Eagle clan, of the nearby village of Auk. Illustrated here is the pole that tells of Raven's cosmic creations and his supernatural powers. The design is based on the well-known original from Wrangell by William Ukas.

At the top of the pole is Raven, standing on the bent-wood box from which he released Sun to give light to the world.

A major characteristic of Raven is his supernatural ability to transform himself into anything at all—quite often a human. The next portrayal of Raven shows his duality in being both bird and human at the same time. The carving has the heads of both, wings as well as arms, while clawed bird legs share space with human legs and feet.

Below is Raven again, complete in bird form, having stolen the Moon and the Stars and thrust them into the sky.

The woman at the base wears a labret and is an all-knowing old woman who can foretell the future. In a Tlingit version of the story of Raven stealing the Sun, carver Edward Kunz recounted that it was she who warned the chief who owned the boxes containing the Sun, Moon and Stars, that Raven was up to no good.

6 ft.
1.8 m

181

113 LOCATION: *Juneau, Alaska—Auk Tribe Building, Village St. and Willoughby Ave.*
CARVER: *Edward Kunz, William Smith, Tom Jimmy, Edward Kunz Jr.*
CULTURAL STYLE: *Tlingit*

The second of two poles in front of the Auk Tribe Building was carved to honour the Eagle clan and comprises their family crests. Edward Kunz provided the identities and details of each. It took the carvers six weeks, working eight hours a day, to complete the pole.

Looking down from the top is a proud Eagle, holding a coho salmon in its claws. This represents a man of the Eagle clan, holding to him his wife of the Coho people of the Raven clan. Beneath Eagle is a slave holding a copper worth ten slaves, and below him is Wolf, sitting upright. At the base is Bear, also sitting up, paws to its chin. The carved face on its stomach, Edward Kunz said, is a way of showing Bear's feelings. Kunz also painted the design on the wall between the two poles.

Juneau has some eighteen totem poles, indoors and out. They are mainly replicas or fairly recent carvings, but one of the oldest and finest is from the late nineteenth century. Originally in the Haida village of Sukkwan, across the channel from Hydaburg, Alaska, it now stands indoors in the main lobby of the State Office Building.

6 ft.
1.8 m

List of Poles by Location

Alert Bay, British Columbia
Poles 74 to 77

Campbell River, British Columbia
Poles 63 to 71

Cape Mudge, British Columbia
Poles 72 and 73

Comox Reserve, British Columbia
Poles 61 and 62

Courtenay, British Columbia
Poles 59 and 60

Departure Bay Ferry Terminal, British Columbia
Pole 57

Douglas border crossing, British Columbia
Pole 1

Duncan, British Columbia
Poles 51 to 55

Hazelton, British Columbia
Pole 94

Horseshoe Bay Ferry Terminal, British Columbia
Pole 35

Juneau, Alaska
Poles 110 to 113

Ketchikan, Alaska
Poles 101 to 104

Kispiox, British Columbia
Poles 95 to 100

Kitsumkalum, British Columbia
Poles 88 and 89

'Ksan, British Columbia
Poles 91, 92 and 93

Nanaimo, British Columbia
Pole 56

Ninstints, British Columbia
Poles 82, 83 and 84

Old Masset, British Columbia
Poles 80 and 81

Port Hardy, British Columbia
Pole 78

Prince Rupert, British Columbia
Poles 85, 86 and 87

Qualicum Beach, British Columbia
Pole 58

Sechelt, British Columbia
Pole 36

Sidney, British Columbia
Pole 39

Skidegate, British Columbia
Pole 79

Swartz Bay Ferry Terminal, British Columbia
Pole 38

Terrace, British Columbia
Pole 90

Tsawwassen Ferry Terminal, British Columbia
Pole 37

Vancouver, British Columbia
Poles 2 to 34

Victoria, British Columbia
Poles 40 to 50

Wrangell, Alaska
Poles 105 to 109

SELECTED READING

Bancroft-Hunt, Norman, and Werner Forman. *People of the Totem*. Toronto: Doubleday; New York: G. P. Putnam's Sons, 1979.

Barbeau, Marius. *Totem Poles*. 2 vols. Anthropological Series no. 30, Bulletin 119. Ottawa: National Museum of Canada, 1964.

Barbeau, Marius. *Totem Poles of the Gitksan, Upper Skeena River, British Columbia*. Anthropological Series no. 12, Bulletin 61. Ottawa: National Museum of Canada, 1973.

Boas, Franz. *Kwakiutl Ethnography*. Ed. Helen Codere. Chicago: University of Chicago Press, 1966.

B.C. Indian Arts Society. *Mungo Martin, Man of Two Cultures*. Sidney, B.C.: Gray's Publishing, 1982.

Clutesi, George. *Potlatch*. Sidney, B.C.: Gray's Publishing, 1969.

Cole, Douglas. *Captured Heritage: The Scramble for Northwest Coast Artifacts*. Vancouver: Douglas & McIntyre; Seattle: University of Washington Press, 1985.

Duff, Wilson, ed. *Histories, Territories and Laws of the Kitwancool*. Anthropology in B.C. memoir no. 4. Victoria: British Columbia Provincial Museum, 1959.

Foster, Scott. *Totem Talk: A Guide to Juneau Totem Poles*. Juneau: Gastineau Channel Centennial Association, 1985.

Garfield, Viola E., and Linn A. Forrest. *The Wolf and the Raven: Totem Poles of Southeastern Alaska*. Seattle: University of Washington Press, 1961.

Halpin, Marjorie M. *Totem Poles: An Illustrated Guide*. Museum Note no. 3. Vancouver: University of British Columbia Press in association with University of British Columbia Museum of Anthropology, 1981.

Hasset, Dawn, and F. W. M. Drew. *Totem Poles of Prince Rupert*. Prince Rupert: Museum of Northern British Columbia, 1982.

Hawthorn, Audrey. *Kwakiutl Art*. Vancouver: Douglas & McIntyre; Seattle: University of Washington, 1967

Holm, Bill. *Smoky-Top: The Art and Times of Willie Seaweed*. Seattle: University of Washington Press; Vancouver: Douglas & McIntyre, 1983.

Jonaitis, Aldona. *From the Land of the Totem Poles: The Northwest Coast Indian Art Collection at the American Museum of Natural History*. New York: American Museum of Natural History/ Seattle: University of Washington Press; Vancouver: Douglas & McIntyre, 1988.

Keithahn, Edward L. *Monuments in Cedar—The Authentic Story of the Totem Poles*. Seattle: Superior Publishing, 1963.

MacDonald, George F. *Haida Monumental Art: Villages of the Queen Charlotte Islands*. Vancouver: University of British Columbia Press, 1983.

MacDonald, George F. *Ninstints*. Vancouver: University of British Columbia, 1983.

McDonald, James. "Su-sit'aatk: The Raising of Two Crest Poles." *Rotunda*. Vol. 21, no. 2 (Fall 1988).

Malin, Edward. *Totem Poles of the Pacific Northwest Coast*. Portland, Oregon: Timber Press, c1986.

Miller, Polly, and Leon Gordon Miller. *The Lost Heritage of Alaska: The Adventures and Art of the Alaskan Coastal Indians*. New York: Bonanza Books, 1967.

Nuytten, Phil. *The Totem Carvers: Charlie James, Ellen Neel and Mungo Martin*. Vancouver: Panorama Publications, 1982.

Reid, Bill. *Out of the Silence*. Amon Carter Museum of Western Art, 1971.

Reid, Bill, and Robert Bringhurst. *The Raven Steals the Light*. Vancouver: Douglas & McIntyre; Seattle: University of Washington Press, 1984.

Steltzer, Ulli. *A Haida Potlatch*. Vancouver: Douglas & McIntyre, 1984.

Stewart, Hilary. *Cedar: Tree of Life to the Northwest Coast Indians*. Vancouver: Douglas & McIntyre; Seattle: University of Washington Press, 1984.

Stewart, Hilary. *Looking at Indian Art of the Northwest Coast*. Vancouver: Douglas & McIntyre; Seattle: University of Washington Press, 1979.

INDEX

189